The Dream That Wouldn't Die

THE 50-YEAR FIGHT FOR PRESTWICK AIRPORT

By Ann Galbraith

ISBN 978-0-9799051-4-8

Published by Exit Zero Publishing, 500 Forrestal Road, Suite Zero,
Rio Grande, NJ 08242, USA
www.exitzero.us

Cover photos (clockwise from top left) courtesy of: The David F.
McIntyre Collection; Mirrorpix; Phil Toman; Phil Toman;
David Townsend; Mirrorpix; www.istock.com

Previous page: 1940s painting by Tom Gilfillan, courtesy of
The David F. McIntyre Collection

Cover and book design by Jack Wright, Exit Zero Publishing

Contents

This book is dedicated to all men of vision...

EARLY morning, April 1, 1992. A small group of men are huddled in the middle of the vast and deserted terminal of Prestwick Airport in Ayrshire. The check-in desks are empty, the shops, restaurants and bars closed. Neglect hangs in the air. Some of the group have been up all night and are exhausted. They regard each other with bewilderment. They have just bought the airport — and most are wondering what on earth they are going to do with it. None has any experience of running a commercial airport, but with a huge investment of belief, barrowloads of determination and no little money, they have succeeded in wresting the struggling terminal from the clutches of a reluctant British Airports Authority. They have rescued it from almost certain closure and hopefully averted the damage such a move would have caused not just to the Ayrshire economy but to Scotland as a whole.

As they await the arrival of the country's media, many of whom, they believe, have contributed to the virtual shutdown of the airport with a relentless campaign of negative and damaging stories and editorials over the past decade, more than one is mulling over the notion that while the first battle has been won, the real fight to secure the airport's future stretches out ahead. Prestwick is handling just six flights a week, — cargo flights, no passengers — one a day except Friday. These are FedEx DC-8s that drop in to refuel in the early hours en route to India with used garments for recycling.

Looking back on that auspicious moment, Ayr businessman Bill Miller, the first non-executive chairman of PIK Limited, the airport's new operating company, said: "It was an act of faith."

Miller, founder and chairman of Prestwick Holdings, one of Scotland's first electronics companies, had played an important part in bringing together the team of mainly Ayrshire businessmen who were to make up the board of the operating company and who were now standing there, nervously surveying their purchase. They were a disparate group. Along with Miller, there was Jim Moffat, head of the leading Scottish travel firm AT Mays; Tim Morrison, who ran a highly-successful family drinks and distillery business and who was based locally in Maybole; Sir David McNee, the former Commissioner of London's Metropolitan Police and before that Chief Constable of Strathclyde Police; and Matthew Hudson, Canadian lawyer, property developer and entrepreneur. Hudson had already contributed a great deal leading up to the purchase and would go on to play a vital part in the airport's future success.

These were the businessmen and investors.

Also included in that early morning group of prime movers were Councillor Ian Welsh of Kyle and Carrick District Council, who had spearheaded a long campaign throughout the 1980s to save the airport from closure; George Giles, a former gen-

Previous page: *photograph courtesy of dmccoy@nildram.co.uk*

Rather than having money to burn, George Younger, Ayr MP and chairman of the Royal Bank Of Scotland, had to conceive a financial plan to support the rescue of Prestwick *Photo courtesy of* Scottish Daily Record

eral manager at the airport in the BAA days and who had an important position as adviser and consultant in the early stages; and Allan MacDonald, Ayr-born general manager of the British Aerospace plant at Prestwick, who had played a major role in facilitating the deal.

Last, but certainly not least, the main power and political influence behind the successful buyout, the man who gave it leadership, clout and gravitas, George Younger, MP for Ayr, former Secretary of State for Scotland and Secretary of State for Defence in the Thatcher government and chairman of the Royal Bank of Scotland. A long-time supporter of the airport – he was later to take the title Lord Younger of Prestwick when he moved to the House of Lords – Younger was about to leave Parliament at the end of a long and successful political career and he did not want to depart with a closed airport in his constituency. In his welcoming remarks to the press he was to speak of a two-year battle to secure the future of the airport.

But the struggle had started long before that.

PIK

Chapter 1
In The
Beginning

IN 1933, two young Scots were major players in the Renfrew-based City of Glasgow Auxiliary Air Force 602 bomber squadron: David Fowler McIntyre and the Marquis of Douglas and Clydesdale. McIntyre had moved to Ayr from Glasgow as a child. At 21 he took his first flying lesson in December 1926, despite the opposition of his family, who were urging him to follow a safer and more secure career in the family docking business. However, within a month, he had completed his first solo flight and proved himself a natural flier, impressing the RAF sufficiently to appoint him to the 602 Squadron, the first British auxiliary squadron to be commissioned after the First World War. He went on to become commanding officer of the squadron's B Flight. Commanding officer of the "C" flight at that time was Douglas Douglas-Hamilton, Marquis of Douglas and Clydesdale, and the two men became firm friends.

In those days of expedition and adventure, Mount Everest was still very much an enigma and the challenge to become the first to fly over the world's highest mountain occupied many a young adventurer's mind. The Houston Mount Everest Flight in 1933, to chart geographic and meteorological features hitherto unknown, was beginning to take shape. McIntyre, recognised as an exceptionally-gifted pilot, was chosen to fly the second plane, earning his place in the face of stiff competition from more experienced officers. It was no coincidence that his friend Douglas Douglas-Hamilton had been appointed chief pilot for the mission.

During the widely-acclaimed adventure, the bond of friendship between the two men strengthened and they realised they shared the same dream of a future in flying. It was only natural that when they returned to the UK they should start looking around for a suitable site for their ambitious plans. Prestwick, despite its comparatively remote situation on the west coast of Scotland, seemed to fit the bill.

Brought up and educated in Ayr, McIntyre knew the area well. In 1934, a few small planes were already using, as a runway, the meadow at the end of Monkton village, a mile or two from Prestwick. As a Renfrew-based pilot, McIntyre knew that aircraft operated by Midland and Scottish Air Ferries Ltd were frequently diverted in bad weather to Monkton from Renfrew Airport, near Glasgow. Around that time, Ayr Town Council had suggested to the neighbouring Prestwick and Monkton councils that they join together to build an airport to serve both communities. But, in the familiar pattern of local authorities since time began, they couldn't agree on a suitable site and the idea was dropped.

An RAF survey in 1934 also gave rise to speculation that a seaplane base was under consideration for Prestwick, but that was denied by the Air Ministry and nothing came of it. Amid the varied speculation, one fact became clear: the site had potential.

It so happened that around that time the British government introduced a scheme for expanding the Royal Air Force — firms were to be given contracts to open flying training schools where young men could do their first 50 hours as civilians before entering the RAF to complete their training as pilots. The scheme appealed

Wing men... David McIntyre and Douglas Douglas-Hamilton at the HQ of Scottish Aviation
Photograph courtesy of the David F. McIntyre Collection

to the two young aviation pioneers and Clydesdale and McIntyre, in association with the de Havilland Aircraft Company, formed Scottish Aviation Ltd at Prestwick in August 1935. They had two principal objectives: to expand air travel and to establish an aircraft industry on the West Coast of Scotland.

The Air Ministry approved their chosen site on the Monkton side of the Pow Burn, just behind Orangefield House, a former private home, dating from 1690. The site enjoyed a fine weather record and McIntyre, having lived in the area, knew it could be clear for flying 365 days a year. The site was not without its opponents, though, and the plan almost fell through when one member of the Air Ministry Aerodromes Board kept insisting that Prestwick was exceptionally unsuitable for flying and training because, he alleged, it had a poor weather record. It later emerged that he had spent part of his childhood in Saltcoats, a town which sits further up the Ayrshire coast in the Greenock rain belt, and he assumed the weather at Prestwick was the same. Eventually, McIntyre convinced the board that the Prestwick area regularly enjoyed 365 days fit for flying training in a year and Scottish Aviation Limited took off.

The success of the flying school was quickly recognised, with a large number of training contracts allotted to Scottish Aviation. As early as 1936, McIntyre saw the potential of the site, predicting: "In 10 years time you will see here an international airport and aircraft industry." He really intended it to happen but it is doubtful anyone believed him at that time. However, the outbreak of war in 1939 was to change everything, and one disorientated pilot was to alter the future of Prestwick Airport forever.

By the time hostilities commenced, the flying school had proven its worth. More than 1,300 pilots and 2,000 navigators had passed through its doors. Scottish Aviation became a Royal Air Force station and David McIntyre was promoted to the title of Officer Commanding, Prestwick. The war, however, meant a parting of the ways for the partners. Douglas-Hamilton took a senior role in the Royal Air Force, taking charge of air defence in Scotland and the Air Training Corps. When Rudolf Hess, Hitler's deputy, flew to Scotland in 1941 he was heading to Douglas-Hamilton's home at Dungavel House, near Strathaven, when he crashed near Eaglesham. Hess had hoped to involve Hamilton in negotiating peace between Britain and Germany.

Douglas-Hamilton and McIntyre never worked together at Prestwick again, but the clouds of war had a silver lining for the airport base as the role of Scottish Aviation expanded. No longer simply a flight training school, the company began manufacturing and servicing aircraft. When a huge Lockheed Hudson from the North Atlantic Ferry Route lost course and touched down at Prestwick one night, it opened up a new role for the small Scottish airport, one which would continue into peacetime. Before Pearl Harbour and the official entry of the United States into the war, an organisation called ATFERO – Atlantic Ferry Organisation – had come into existence for the supply, by air, of American-built bombers. After an overland trip from California to Canada, the planes flew to the United Kingdom in what was to become known as the Atlantic Ferry service. This was the US contribution to the war in Europe agreed by President Roosevelt and Prime Minister Winston Churchill.

Initially, the established RAF station at Aldergrove in Ireland was the chosen UK base but on November 29, 1940, when a formation from Gander in Newfoundland, Canada, was en route to Aldergrove, Captain EPM Eves lost contact with his fellow pilots and landed at Prestwick. He walked over to the duty pilot's office to report, saying he had completed a flight of 10 hours 54 minutes and had come from Gander.

"Seems a long flight," said the duty pilot. "Where's Gander?"

That chance landing had repercussions that reverberate today. Prestwick was soon named the main terminal for all aircraft flying from Canada, and later from the

An aerial view of Prestwick aerodrome during World War Two
Photograph courtesy of the David F. McIntyre Collection

US, throughout the war. This service was to put the previously-unknown Prestwick Airport firmly on the international aviation map. The airport was requisitioned by the Air Ministry in 1941 as part of the war effort, though Scottish Aviation continued to carry the station operating contract. To cater for the increase in traffic a new runway was built which, with amazing foresight, David McIntyre insisted should be 2,200 yards long and 100 yards wide – almost twice the Air Ministry standard size. As a pilot, he recognised this exceptional width would give tired pilots an easier landing option after a long Atlantic crossing.

The peak month for aircraft movements during the war was August 1944, when 7,847 were logged and during the period 1941-45 it is estimated there were 37,000 aircraft movements through Prestwick. The war proved conclusively that the Atlantic could be crossed safely on a regular basis in summer and winter.

As peacetime dawned, Scottish Aviation Ltd, under McIntyre's leadership, had a major foothold in the British aviation industry – a position, his son Dougal says in his book *Prestwick's Pioneer*, the post-war British government seemed determined to deny and obstruct at every opportunity. The town council of Prestwick, however, recognised the impact the development of the airport had had on the local community and conferred the freedom of the town on both McIntyre and the Duke of Hamilton in June 1945.

The success of Prestwick as an international airport, though, was another matter. So impressed was the new Ministry of Civil Aviation that, in a shock move, it declared itself the landlord of the airport and took the station licence from Scottish Aviation and its founder, thus separating the future development of the airport and the aircraft factory.

A long and painful legal battle followed. In 1947, the Ministry offered £87,000 for the compulsory purchase of the airport, despite a valuation of £300,000, and it was not until six years later that the airport was finally bought by the Government from a reluctant David McIntyre. Scottish Aviation had fought long and hard against the compulsory purchase, but after years of protracted negotiations over rent allegedly due for the wartime period, as well as compensation, the Ministry finally paid £450,000 and Scottish Aviation acquired a 99-year lease which allowed them to keep operating the aircraft factory site and access to the runway – an agreement that was to play a vital role in saving the airport from closure 40 years later.

The end of the war brought euphoria and a resumption of normal life. For the aircraft companies that meant one thing: commercial flights and holiday travel. With the end of the war in Japan that August came the release of some aircraft to TWA, Pan American and American Overseas Airlines for the start of commercial transAtlantic services. The first test flights duly landed at Prestwick in September and October. Prestwick was designated Britain's second international airport after Heathrow on April 1, 1946, and in the May scheduled transatlantic flights began through Prestwick with the arrival of a KLM DCV4 from Amsterdam on its way to New York.

David McIntyre had applied in May 1944 for the right to operate transatlantic and European passenger routes from Prestwick and had been granted permission to obtain and convert aircraft for their own use in late 1945. His Scottish Airlines company launched a service to Belfast in January 1946 and, despite post-war fuel restrictions, they also operated a service to London – but not for long. The newly-elected Labour government had other plans and they lost little time in introducing their nationalisation policies. In August 1946, Scottish Airlines were barred from operating scheduled passenger services, which were by this time only legally permitted by the monopoly British European Airways and British Overseas Airways Corporation. McIntyre opposed this further government intervention into his business and complained bitterly at BEA stopping their London-Prestwick service.

By October 1946, McIntyre's Belfast service was also grounded. By dogged perseverance, he got the route restarted by the December but spent fruitless years lobbying the Government to recognise the value of his Scottish Airlines flights. The small matter of the battle still waging over the compulsory purchase of the airport and his fight for compensation were almost certainly factors working against his interest. He was never allowed to compete on an even playing field, presaging events that were to follow almost 40 years later.

Throughout the 1950s and early 1960s the airport was busy with passenger and freight flights. Within five years of the war ending there were 79 weekly summer

Elvis Presley's only confirmed touch-down on British soil was at Prestwick on his way to the States from a US Army base in Germany in March 1960 *(c) Newsquest Media Group - used with permission*

scheduled transatlantic services through Prestwick by major airlines — KLM flew 27, BOAC 12, TCA seven, AOA seven, and Air France three. In addition, a stream of new services flew to Lisbon, Copenhagen, Brussels and Oslo. Icelandic Airways flew Reykjavik-Prestwick-London services in 1949 and two years later, the latest state-of-the-art aircraft, the Comet and the Brabazon, touched down at the airport.

In 1952 the United States Air Force formed its Air-Sea Rescue Base at Prestwick and building work started at Greensite, on the fringe of the airport. In 1960 the transatlantic gateway status granted 14 years earlier was confirmed by the Government's White Paper on Civil Aerodromes.

Prestwick was Scotland's official transcontinental airport, and the times were good. These were the star-studded glamour days for the airport. Air travel was growing more popular and affordable as Britain emerged from the austerity of war. People had television, were going to the cinema and were more aware of the big wide world awaiting them. They wanted to travel abroad instead of holidaying at home. The British seaside resorts and weather were losing their appeal — two weeks on the Costa del Sol were more appealing than the rain-drenched promenades of Blackpool. The sun-kissed shores of the Mediterranean and the Americas beckoned. The package holiday market flourished as people realised it was not just the rich and famous who could fly to exotic destinations — and Prestwick enjoyed its share of the rich and famous. On his way back to America in 1960, after serving with the US Air

Before the days of a stand-alone air traffic control tower at Prestwick, an improvised extension to Orangefield House Hotel was the airport's nerve centre *Crown Copyright: RCAHMS*

Force in Germany, Elvis Presley stopped over at the neighbouring Greeensite USAF base, famously the only UK visit he would ever make. Word of his arrival spread, and the crowds gathered at the base perimeter, local girls screaming hysterically as they caught a glimpse of their hero. Presley signed autographs, posed for pictures as his aircraft was being refuelled – and then it was back to the US.

The glitterati were regularly photographed wafting through the terminal building, the former Orangefield House, en route to more exotic destinations. Film and sports star pictures lined the walls. Hollywood superstars Bob Hope, Bing Crosby, Judy Garland, Frank Sinatra, Alfred Hitchcock and Stewart Granger were among those caught on camera as they passed through. Roy Rogers and his equally famous horse Trigger were piped into the terminal – a bagpipe welcome was one of the hospitality highlights of landing at Prestwick.

The small airport hotel, which formed part of the terminal, with its distinctive control tower on the roof, was THE place to be seen for the locals. The airport had been enlarged and improved in the war years when it was taken over by the Air Ministry and by the end of the war it had become arguably the best-equipped and most active terminal in Europe. The reception walls and lounge were decorated with a series of colourful panels depicting aviation scenes from across the world by local artist Tom Gilfillan. The hotel restaurant was where the Ayrshire smart set went in the days before nightclubs, when the pubs and dance halls closed well before midnight and there were no late-night takeaways. The dining room, with its elegant French doors and worldwide reputation, was open 24 hours a day to cater for transatlantic passengers. It was the done thing to drive out there for breakfast in the small hours after attending a dance or a night at the theatre. Midnight or 4am, the welcome was always the same. The scrambled eggs became a thing of legend with local customers who, sober or tipsy, received silver service star treatment at tables resplendent in starched white linen tablecloths and napkins.

An important new chapter opened when Ayr District Licensing Court made Prestwick the first UK airport to sell duty-free whisky. Until that point, all the major international airports in Europe had enjoyed the benefits of duty-free sales and passengers were by-passing Prestwick to take advantage – particularly at Shannon Airport in Ireland. The Duty-Free Centre was officially opened in 1959 by Glasgow millionaire draper Hugh Fraser, later Lord Fraser of Allander, who went on to own Harrods in London, making it part of his House of Fraser empire.

But by 1960 it was obvious that the days of the traditional airport were numbered. Celebrating 25 years in service, Prestwick was getting busier and a £4million upgrade was scheduled. The demand for air travel was continuing to grow and bigger, better facilities were needed. The government announced plans for a new terminal building, new freight building, an extension to the main runway and a new control tower. Orangefield House was demolished in 1966.

The new terminal was good news for airline passengers but the new plans were also welcomed by local drivers as they included a new loop road round the airport which meant they would no longer be held up by barriers and flashing lights where the old road crossed the runway.

Construction work on the new terminal began in June 1961 and when it was officially opened by Queen Elizabeth, the Queen Mother, in September 1964, Ayrshire witnessed its biggest social event for decades as the great and the good packed into a special reception in the terminal building after the ceremony. One local newspaper reporter recorded what she noticed most from the occasion was the smell of mothballs – the local gentry having raided their wardrobes for their furs and finery.

The new glass-and-chrome terminal was the envy of the country. It even had provision at the north end for a covered link to a potential railway station on the main Ayr-Glasgow line which ran past the airport – though that option was not exercised until almost three decades later. There were check-in desks for all the major airlines: British Airways, British Caledonian, KLM, SAS, Air Canada, PamAm and the Canadian charter Wardair. It was also one of the first terminals built to meet the demands of the new jet age traveller – there was a bank, post office, shops, a first-class restaurant, cafeteria, bars and a large duty-free shop. An underground refuelling system was also installed. There were plans for a new hotel but these never came to fruition.

THE year 1966 saw major change at Prestwick. That was when the airport came under the ownership of the newly-formed British Airports Authority. This was also the year that the new Glasgow Abbotsinch Airport was built as a replacement for Renfrew. The plan was that Glasgow would be used for short and medium-haul flights and Prestwick would keep its transatlantic status.

Prestwick was seen as a rival to Heathrow in those early, heady days as a natural gateway to Europe. There were few weather constraints, since it was virtually fog-free all year, as McIntyre had predicted. It had two major runways, one of which was among the longest in the country, thanks again to the foresight of McIntyre. There were no environmental or noise problems and no stacking or slot problems. It was capable of being a global gateway for wide-body flights from anywhere in the world and there was plenty of space for airport-related and commercial development. No other airport in Britain boasted such facilities.

The 1970s were particularly successful for Prestwick which, by this time, was handling 500,000 passengers a year and employing around 1,500 people. The first Boeing 747 jumbo arrived in 1970 and in June 1971 the spectators' gallery was packed as Concorde gave her first low-level flying display in Scotland. In the summer of 1972 Prestwick was scheduled by BOAC to become the third busiest airport after Heathrow and JFK in New York, in their global network of 77 cities. BOAC and BEA merged to become British Airways in 1973 and the summer of that year saw 105,000 passengers using British Airways out of Prestwick. Concorde landed at Prestwick for the first time and continued to make many visits throughout the years. British Caledonian's first scheduled transatlantic service went into operation the same year.

The first blip in the success story came in 1974 when a jump in world oil prices saw a reduction in passengers, leading PanAm to withdraw their flights. Weathering the setback, the airport continued to thrive and, in 1977 when Scottish Aviation's aircraft factory was nationalised and became part of British Aerospace, the Bermuda 2 agreement saw Prestwick designated as the official gateway between the USA and Scotland. A further boost came with the news that Northwest Airlines were introducing a daily scheduled service – Seattle-Minneapolis-Boston-Prestwick-Copenhagen.

In 1980 Laker Airways was granted a licence to operate direct scheduled low-fare services to Los Angeles and Miami, an expansion of Sir Freddie Laker's hugely-successful Skytrain out of Gatwick. Flying Tigers, the world's largest air cargo carrier, revealed plans to launch a weekly scheduled service to New York during 1981.

Like the 1970s, the 1980s started off full of promise – but the optimism was short-lived. A review by BAA in 1978-79 had re-affirmed Prestwick's place as Scotland's transatlantic gateway – all Scottish flights to Canada and the USA would fly solely from Ayrshire, a status reinforced by a further review conducted by the House of Commons Select Committee on Scottish Affairs. But the continuing expansion of Glasgow Airport was beginning to affect Prestwick's growth. Gateway status was a fine concept, but it was not being backed up by connecting domestic or continental services. These all flew from Glasgow, and there was no link, no working partnership between the two airports. Passengers arriving at Prestwick could not fly on anywhere else. It was a dead end.

Then in 1981, completely out of the blue, British Airways, Prestwick's biggest and most prestigious customer, announced it was moving all its business, passenger and freight, to Glasgow. Although other airlines stayed loyal, alarm bells began to ring. Jim Harris, head of the UK and Ireland division of BA, travelled to Prestwick to address the 65 employees who were to lose their jobs. The move to Glasgow, he said, was to stem the company's overall losses which would have been less, he claimed, if the transatlantic flights had been able to operate from Glasgow. British Airways eventually moved out in August 1983. A further blow to the airport was the collapse of Freddie Laker's empire in 1982.

Glasgow Airport was now seen as a competitor rather than a complementary service and, more importantly, for the first time it was seen as a threat. The first signs were appearing that Glasgow was after the lucrative transatlantic business. By 1983 serious discussions were also taking place between BAA, the City of London and Whitehall regarding the privatisation of the airport authority, privatisation being one of the main political platforms of the Thatcher government of the day. In 1985-86 a further review of Scottish Lowland Airports Policy was carried out and yet again the Tory government confirmed its support for Prestwick. However, a 1985 government White Paper carried a warning that they were looking for an improvement in Prestwick's performance by 1989, or there would need to be another review. In 1985, the airport recorded a trading loss of £2.5million.

The Scottish Airport Division of BAA had been set up in 1975 and for many years the profits from Prestwick had subsidised the other Scottish airports at Glasgow, Edinburgh and Aberdeen. Now it was in trouble. When the government was examining how best to privatise BAA, the authority argued strongly that the Scottish airports should be kept together as a division of BAA rather than being privatised separately, that the monopoly ownership should be maintained. Although this plan drew criticism, BAA won the argument and was privatised as one unit in 1987. With the monopoly of ownership came one valuable asset: land. And Prestwick, with 300 acres, had plenty. In response to a Parliamentary written question in November 1989, Patrick McLoughlin, the Aviation Minister said: "The prospectus issued when BAA plc shares were offered for sale noted that of the 1815 acres, 938 were at BAA's Scottish airports, predominantly at Prestwick."

After privatisation in 1987, the bulk of the property assets, including Prestwick's 300 acres, were transferred to Lynton plc, a property company purchased by BAA the same year. Although the exact value of the land is not noted, the total value of land and buildings at Prestwick at that time amounted to £27.5 million. Concerned observers saw this as Prestwick's assets being stripped to the benefit of the overall balance sheet of the company, rather than to the benefit of the airport. A Labour Party review at the time said: "Having achieved its goal of securing ownership of Prestwick and the other Scottish Airports following privatisation, in order to take control of valuable land and property, BAA plc no longer has any use for Prestwick. This is the danger of monopoly owners. As far as BAA is concerned Prestwick can close. Prestwick is simply not safe in BAA's hands."

PIK

Chapter 2
Open Skies
Close the Door

COUNCILLOR Ian Welsh first began feeling concerned about the future of Prestwick Airport as early as 1984, three years before the privatisation of BAA and just after the major transfer of British Airways to Glasgow. An assistant head teacher at Auchinleck Academy in East Ayrshire, Welsh was Prestwick born-and-bred — his family home had bordered the airport runway and as a child he would stand in his back garden and watch the planes taking off.

A Labour Party member and activist, he had just been elected to Kyle and Carrick District Council and as he represented the town of Prestwick, it followed that he should also be the council's representative on the Prestwick Airport Consultative Committee, a group of committed and interested individuals who met once a month to keep an eye on developments at the airport. The committee had been formed in the 1970s and its role was formally described as being "to represent the interests of the community and users in the preservation and enhancement of Prestwick Airport as an international gateway, in keeping with its history and commensurate with its well-founded reputation for offering the best weather on a year-round basis of all the international airports in Europe". Meetings were taken seriously by the BAA management and were normally attended by the airport's general manager.

Because the 1985-86 Lowland Airports Review had come out in favour once again of Prestwick as the transatlantic gateway, there was a feeling of optimism. However the demands from Glasgow Airport for transatlantic flights were getting louder by the month. A well-publicised attempt by British Midland to fly direct from Glasgow to New York in 1982 had been thwarted. The licence was approved by the Civil Aviation Authority but BAA appealed to the government and the licence was quashed. However, Prestwick supporters realised this was a sign of things to come and they had to be prepared to fight further moves to remove Prestwick's sole right to transatlantic services.

With admirable foresight, Ian Welsh decided some direct action was needed, a sort of pre-emptive strike, and in his role as councillor he launched a Keep Prestwick Flying initiative. This was directed at bringing home to the local community, the Labour Party in Scotland, which controlled most local authorities, and the government, just how important it was that Prestwick should, as his slogan said, keep flying. Soon cars all over the district sported stickers on their rear windows bearing the campaign slogan. Through this campaign he wanted to ram home the point that Prestwick had to keep its gateway status. After all, it had no European flights. The airport was a lynchpin of the local economy with around 900 jobs directly related to the airport, not to mention the thousands more linked to the aircraft industries, British Aerospace (the former Scottish Aviation Ltd) and Caledonian Airmotive. These two companies would not stay long at Prestwick, he argued, if there were a threat to the future of the airport.

With his team of supporters, Councillor Welsh trawled around all the local summer events, issuing thousands of car stickers. The end result was a 3,000-name petition which was taken to the Department of Transport in London. Around the same time, with all the talk of future reviews and pressure growing from the Glasgow Airport lobby, workers at Prestwick Airport were beginning to get nervous for their jobs and this led to the formation of a parallel campaign group, the Prestwick Gateway Action Committee. A local airport supporter and stalwart, Sam Milliken, had first come to Prestwick in 1963 as a customs officer and on his arrival he was greeted by colleagues with the surprising words: "What have you come here for? Don't you know we are closing down?"

The airport obviously survived those initial fears, but by 1983 Milliken felt closure could be on the horizon. The situation had become acute with the transfer of British Airways and staff began to be seriously worried about their future security. "They were in a difficult situation," said Milliken. "They worked for BAA and felt they couldn't speak out, fearing for their jobs. Staff working for the airlines were in a similar situation. They all shared the same fear — they all felt BAA wanted to shut the place down and move everything to Glasgow."

By 1985 the situation had not improved. Milliken was about to retire and as he was a civil servant felt it was easier for him to operate as an effective activist. With the support of his colleagues and the permission of George Giles, Prestwick's general manager, he called a meeting in the concourse of the terminal and was encouraged to see 200 turn up. By coincidence, the Scottish Airports boss, Gordon Watson, was arriving off a plane at the same time, from a sales mission to the USA. He was told about the meeting.

"He wasn't pleased," said Milliken, "But there was nothing he could do about it." So the Gateway Action Committee was born with Milliken as convener. A working committee was formed and the group had the full support, in a rare show of unity of both the local MPs: Conservative George Younger, who was then Secretary of State for Scotland, and Labour's George Foulkes, who represented the neighbouring Carrick Cumnock and Doon Valley constituency. Local business people as well as airport staff members were also represented. "It was obvious to everyone that BAA were trying to run the place down," said Milliken. "We felt we had to do something about it."

It was made clear at the start that the committee was non-political, although it had the support of the MPs, and it remained so throughout its existence. Six months after the committee was formed, BAA invited Milliken to become secretary of the Airport Consultative Committee. Local businessman Bill Miller, who was to play an important role in the airport's future, was chairman at that time and this meant both had access to information about what was going on at the airport. The action committee got together regularly, and a later meeting in the concourse attracted 400 people, who had the opportunity to grill the new Scottish Airports boss, Vernon Murphy. They wrote to national and local

A publicity photo for Highland Express... but the airline never really got off the ground

newspapers stressing the importance of Prestwick Airport, conducted radio and TV interviews and were in constant touch with George Younger, who they felt had the ear of Mrs Thatcher and influence in government decisions. "We virtually had an open line to Mr Younger," said Milliken. "We could contact him anywhere at any time."

Amidst all the campaigning and closure fears, a ray of hope appeared on the horizon. Bill Miller, the consultative committee chairman, had always said that for Prestwick to survive it was essential to find its own resident airline. Now it looked as if that might be possible. Enter Randolph Fields and Highland Express.

Although only 33, the larger-than-life American lawyer had a proven track record in the airline business. He had helped found Virgin Atlantic in partnership with Richard Branson and, having sold his stake in that business, he wanted to start a similar operation out of Prestwick. Fields burst on to the Ayrshire scene in 1986 like a breath of fresh air, his optimism and enthusiasm just what the beleaguered airport needed. A new airline could see it moving into profit again. The concept would be the same as the highly-successful Virgin formula: cut-price transatlantic flights aimed at the lucrative VFR market – visiting friends and relatives. Fields had seen it work with Virgin, which had earned a pre-tax profit of £2million in its first year on a turnover of £35 million, and was convinced it would succeed in Scotland. Prestwick would be the hub for his new Highland Express airline but passengers would also come from the Midlands, utilising Standsted and Birmingham airports, the latter being a large VFR area that was not well served through London.

Fields wanted to offer low-cost direct flights to North America to a section of the public he felt had been ignored by other airlines and the plan was to use regional airports, an idea well ahead of its time.

Flamboyant American lawyer Randolph Fields had a dream for Prestwick Airport, but ran out of luck
Photograph courtesy of Mirrorpix

Fields was quoted as saying: "The lucky people of the southeast have enjoyed such opportunities for a considerable time; now it is the chance of the people of Scotland and the Midlands." The backers of the concept also saw it as an opportunity to develop Scotland's international trade, particularly the electronics industry, which was enjoying steady growth in Scotland through the 1980s. The market was certainly there, but initially the money was not. Randolph Fields' first effort was grounded in April 1986 due to lack of financial backing. He needed £5 million to get the airline off the ground but perhaps scared off by the financial crash landing of Freddie Laker in 1982, potential backers did not come forward in sufficient numbers and he failed in his plan by a tantalising £500,000.

However, support was strong within the Scottish business community and Fields decided to try again. By the end of the year the scheme was up and running despite the sudden withdrawal of £1million promised by British Coal Enterprise Limited — a decision taken, apparently, because the consortium setting up the airline was headed by the colourful Sir Ian MacGregor, formerly chairman of British Coal and good friend of Margaret Thatcher. MacGregor was blamed by many for destroying the British mining industry and memories were still strong of the disastrous miners' strike of two years earlier. Officially, BCEL said the proposal did not represent an investment they felt able to recommend to the National Coal Board for approval. But everyone believed it was because of the MacGregor connection. Randolph Fields personally guaranteed to cover the missing £1 million while George Younger, fellow Conservative Cabinet member Malcolm Rifkind MP and a number of other influential politicians and business people tried to persuade the Coal Board to change their mind, without success. The Bank of Scotland and the Scottish Office made a concerted effort to secure funds from the European Coal and Steel Community, also without success.

Bill Miller at the time was also vice-chairman of the Scottish CBI and an enthusiastic supporter of Highland Express from its inception. He was happy to join the board and put money into the venture. Miller was founder of Prestwick Holdings, the first publicly-held Scottish hi-tech company. He was managing director and then chairman, a post he held until 1992. Also represented on the board were leading chartered accountants Arthur Andersen, who had worked on the business plan, and Dutchman Peter de Vink, who ran the Edinburgh-based finance house Edinburgh Financial and General Holdings. So by early 1987 they had the cash and the CAA had approved the licence. Highland Express was ready for take-off. Well nearly.

Randolph Fields had vision, but he didn't have luck, that other vital ingredient for the successful entrepreneur. The plan for Highland Express, bold and adventurous as it was, seemed to have the fates against it from the start. The delay in raising the cash meant that Fields had to drastically change his plans.

Originally the business plan featured two Tri-stars, which were very cheap and parked somewhere in the Arizona desert early in 1986. The recession in 1985 had hit the airline industry hard and resulted in many planes becoming surplus to requirements. However, by 1987 the industry had picked up again and the Tri-stars were not available. All that was on offer was one plane – a Boeing 747 which was sold to Highland Express as airworthy and with all the required documentation in place. It soon became clear, however, that the plane was anything but airworthy. When the investors took delivery, the aircraft doors were missing. It had been heavily cannibalised while out of commission, the paperwork was out of date and they had to spend £3 million and precious time getting it ready to fly. That £3 million was almost all the fledgling airline's working capital.

This further delay meant they had the embarrassment of having to cancel the inaugural flight from Prestwick to New York, with the inevitable bad publicity. The flight had been scheduled for May 30. Pipers had been laid on, the champagne had been ordered and invitations had gone out to VIP guests and the media. The press had a field day (pardon the pun) as Fields and his board fumed at the damage to the young company's credibility, not to mention the loss of cash, along with advance bookings. A new launch date was set for June 30 and engineers worked around the clock to get the B747 airworthy.

When Highland Express was launched in a blaze of publicity in the February it had boasted a number of firsts for Scottish travellers. Included in the ticket price was free coach travel to Prestwick from all major Scottish cities and towns through a deal with Scottish City Link coaches. For those travelling to the airport by car there was free parking and business class passengers were offered a complimentary limousine service from home to airport and vice-versa on the return journey. There were games and treats for children, including free ice cream, but there was also a child-free zone on the plane for passengers who didn't want their peace disturbed during the flight. They boasted the lowest fares offered by a scheduled carrier and all seats were bookable in advance.

Everything the passenger could want, except the most important thing: reliability. The one-month delay hit bookings hard and the group lost a lot of lucrative summer traffic. They had also lost their credibility within the travel trade and the press, which stemmed from cancelled flights, changing schedules and broken promises. Desperate efforts had to be made to attract additional funding, but again Lady Luck dealt them a bad hand in the form of Black Monday, October 19, 1987, when share prices around the globe nosedived. A backer in San Francisco, Bill Hambrecht of Hambrecht and Quist, an investment bank which had been a shareholder in the People's Express, was hit hard and had to pull out of a promised investment deal. If that wasn't enough, Highland Express was one of the airlines featured in a free-flights fiasco in which so many customers took up a deal for free trips to the US that the promoting company could not cope and thousands of disappointed passengers didn't get their flights. By the end of the year it was obvious Highland Express was not going to succeed. Losses were already topping £8 million and the receivers were called in. The company was wound up on December 11, 1987. There were 4,000 advance bookings on the day of liquidation.

George Giles, Prestwick Airport's general manager, said at the time: "I was not very popular with the managing director of BAA plc on the morning of the last Highland Express flight into Prestwick. He was annoyed I had not placed a lien on the aircraft preventing its departure to Maastricht as BAA were owed a great deal of money."

The Highland Express crash bit deeply into the airport's financial position in the vital time leading up to the 1989 review. A legal action was raised against Citicorp Industrial Credit, who had provided the faulty plane. The creditors ultimately got cash but the shareholders got nothing. "The Receivers eventually got $250,000 in compensation for the delivery of a plane wrongly described. Ironically, if we had had that money the airline would have survived and Prestwick might not have been in trouble," said Bill Miller.

IT WAS rapidly becoming clear to the Prestwick supporters that they were running against a fast-growing tide of opposition. Following the privatisation of BAA in 1987, the backers of Glasgow Airport had stepped up their campaign for Prestwick to lose its transatlantic monopoly. Glasgow campaigners had the backing of the powerful city business community, the Glasgow Chamber of Commerce and the Scottish press.

The airport made an operating loss of £2.1million in 1988 and as the 1989 review loomed, the real battle for the future of Prestwick was beginning.

Open Skies, the two words Prestwick workers and supporters dreaded most, started being bandied about freely that year. Open Skies meant the freedom of choice for airlines to fly from wherever they wanted and Prestwick supporters knew this could mean the end of the road for the airport's protected Transatlantic Gateway status. With the short-haul national and European traffic increasing at Glasgow, not to mention Edinburgh Airport expanding on the east coast, the prospect of an Open Skies policy was a serious threat to the airport. It could lose all its passenger traffic if the remaining big carriers, in particular Air Canada and Northwest Airlines, chose to move to Glasgow. There had been threats and false alarms in the past but now it really looked as if the supporters' worst fears might be realised. Prestwick could close.

Ironically, the talk of Open Skies had started as the result of a bizarre move by the government as part of its Lowland Airports Review, intended to protect Prestwick. Through the Traffic Distribution Rules 1989, the government had said that while Prestwick could keep its transatlantic status, Glasgow could also have intercontinental flights, but that they had to touch down at Prestwick

(30 miles away) before heading across the Atlantic. Likewise, on the way back they had to stop at the Ayrshire airport before landing again at Glasgow. It was obvious from the start this was not going to work. It was costing the airlines money and sometimes a change of crew – only 15 minutes into a flight.

There were inevitable mix-ups. The tabloids went to town with numerous stories of people arriving at Prestwick to join flights which had started at Glasgow and not being able to get on the plane. Confusion reigned. In fact John Boyle, who headed the big air charter company Air 2000, went to court twice during 1989 to challenge the traffic distribution rules. Boyle, who later went on to start Direct Holidays and become an avid supporter of Prestwick, had decided to fly in the face of the new ruling and launched his programme of summer 1989 flights direct from Glasgow to Orlando in Florida. He had estimated that landing at Prestwick would cost him an extra quarter of a million pounds a year – a price he was not prepared to pay, and he decided his flights would go direct. While legal action to stop him was continuing in the courts, the direct Florida flights were eventually quietly withdrawn because of lack of demand, but the damage to Prestwick's sole right to fly transatlantic had been done.

The Open Skies discussion with the Tory government began in earnest, promoted by BAA and supported by what became known in Prestwick circles as the Glasgow mafia: the city's Chamber of Commerce. Ian Welsh colourfully described them as "a junta of businessmen; storm troopers in pinstriped suits". They were lobbying hard with the Transport Minister Cecil Parkinson and the new Secretary of State for Scotland, Malcolm Rifkind. George Younger had by this time moved on from the Scottish Office to become Defence Secretary, though he was still fighting Prestwick's corner.

Businessmen and women wanted to fly from Glasgow, the chamber claimed, and the mantra they adopted was that Prestwick was too far away, too remote. Maybe the right airport, but in the wrong place. Their claims were not backed up by facts. Travelling to Prestwick was as easy and, in some cases, easier than getting to Glasgow Airport through a congested city. Glasgow had no direct rail or bus link, while passengers could reach Prestwick from Glasgow in less than an hour. The journey from the city centre to city airport could sometimes take as long.

However, the great perception of the too-remote Prestwick was skilfully built up, with the help of the Glasgow-based media. *The Glasgow Herald* put its weight behind the Glasgow Airport campaign, as did its sister paper *The Evening Times* and the *Daily Record*. They printed all the propaganda fed to them by the business lobby at the time. It was a brilliant and skilfully-crafted piece of PR: you say something often enough and eventually people believe it.

Looking at the position rationally – and few did at this time – travelling from Glasgow city centre to Prestwick was no further to travel time-wise than say the City of London to Gatwick, and travellers, particularly those from the US, thought nothing of a one-hour trip from airport to city centre. But no one was listening to the argument coming up from Ayrshire. Campaigners claimed their pro-Prestwick press releases were being binned. The letters columns of the Glasgow newspapers, bombarded over the years with correspondents putting the case for Prestwick, gave perhaps a truer picture of the popular feeling.

Kyle and Carrick District Council now moved up a gear and Prestwick Airport Steering Group was formed. The battle was on to defeat the Open Skies proposal. The steering group was also cross-party — the chairman was Councillor Welsh and members included MPs George Younger and George Foulkes, Tory District Councillor Murray Tosh, Labour Councillor John Baillie of Strathclyde Regional Council and representatives of the business community and trade unions, along with users of the airport. The co-ordinator was Eddie Clark, the district council estates manager who had been seconded from his job to concentrate on building the case for saving the gateway status and preparing their vital submission on Scottish Lowland Airports Policy which was to go to Cecil Parkinson at the Ministry of Transport.

"I had a feeling by then that BAA plc had different plans for the airport," said Councillor Welsh. "I started to feel the corporate strategy was to support Open Skies and at that stage the longer-term strategy was to mothball the airport, though this was denied at the time."

His fear was heightened by a quote from BAA chairman Sir Norman Payne, who said in an interview in *The Times* that if Open Skies were to be given the go-ahead, Prestwick would close as a passenger airport.

Welsh worked closely with George Younger throughout the campaign, despite their political differences. During 1989, Younger had been busy announcing a £100 million transport development strategy for Ayrshire, including the upgrading of the A77 between Ayr and Glasgow, which was seen as good for the future of the airport.

"Unfortunately this proved illusory," said Welsh. (The final upgrading of the A77 to dual carriageway and motorway status between Glasgow and Prestwick Airport was eventually completed in April 2005.)

As the concerted campaign against Prestwick grew, the council and other supporting groups went into overdrive, arranging meetings with staff at the airport and businessmen in the private sector, who at that stage showed little interest in putting up any cash to help save the airport. They lobbied politicians on all sides. John Prestcott, Shadow Transport Secretary, entered into the fray. He was contacted by campaigners who invited him to address a massed meeting of workers at the airport. He promised Labour's support for Prestwick and after he left the platform he said to Willie Poole, the airport unions convener, that he was surprised that with a railway line running alongside the airport, there was no rail stop. He was to return again in 1997, once the rail station was built, and was heard to say to by then engineering manager Willie Poole: "I see you listened to me, then."

Welsh was still assistant head teacher at Auchinleck Academy at this time and his whole life outside work was by now involved in the campaign to save the airport. He said: "My family forgot what I looked like. I would have meetings early morning – 5am wasn't unheard of – go to work, then have meetings at night. We galvanised the whole community, with support from across the country. We commissioned consultants to look at all aspects of the argument for keeping Prestwick's Gateway status. I even co-wrote the Tory party paper putting the Case for Prestwick and had to hide from the TV cameras at the press launch in case any of my Labour Party colleagues saw me. I pretended to tie my shoelaces as the TV cameras panned round!"

As the Glasgow-Prestwick split widened, so did the support within the Labour party in Scotland. Officially in support of Prestwick, Glasgow MPs and councillors broke ranks and spoke out in the press in favour of Open Skies and transatlantic flights from Glasgow. The giant Strathclyde Regional Council also had an established policy to support Prestwick but were being swayed towards Glasgow. It was war.

PIK

Chapter 3
The Case For
Prestwick

I T MADE for heavy reading, but the campaigners thought they had done a good job. Their submission to the Ministry of Transport ran to thousands of pages. In it, the steering group built up the strongest case possible for the retention of the transatlantic flights and they spoke about the passions that had been aroused in Scotland over the future of the airport. A Systems Three survey showed the Scottish people supported the retention of Prestwick as a Transatlantic Gateway. The group argued the wider view — that Prestwick served the whole of Scotland not just the principal cities. They argued there was no concrete evidence that Open Skies would bring an economic benefit to Scotland and that there would be no increase in tourism. Americans, in particular, didn't mind where they landed as they looked on Scotland as a small country. In fact, the group argued, charter passengers preferred to land at Prestwick. The operation of Prestwick as a freight-only airport — one option that had been suggested — would not be feasible, they said, despite the fact that in 1989 the airport was one of the busiest freight handlers in the country. David Mullin, Fed-Ex regional manager for Scotland and Northern Ireland, supported this stand. He said in his submission that there was no evidence of any airport anywhere in the world that could exist on air freight traffic alone.

There were warnings that Scottish industry would suffer and this was backed up by letters from companies big and small. There were the giants that used the airport, including Unysis, Digital, Volvo Trucks and small businesses such as Harkin Seafoods who imported lobsters from Canada and who warned that any delays involved in having to land in Glasgow would have a serious effect on their business as there had to be a quick clearance through customs and transfer to tanks in Ayr. The submission argued that the airport was on the verge of making a profit, that passenger numbers were rising and that the 1987-88 loss of £2.1 million had included £750,000 lost in the collapse of Highland Express. It would cost £27 million to bring Glasgow up to standard with a new terminal and freight facilities, they said. The runway at Glasgow, which BAA admitted would never be as good as Prestwick's, also needed upgrading. The group pointed out Prestwick's better weather record and the number of planes that regularly had to be diverted there. Even Prime Minister Margaret Thatcher had been quoted as saying: "I think we'll find it difficult to do without Prestwick. Prestwick is open when other airports aren't."

They went big on the safety issue. At that time pilots were not happy flying the Atlantic with newly-introduced, twin-engine aircraft, whose use had required them to plan their route so as to be no more than 90 minutes away from diversion airports in Ireland, Iceland, Greenland and Newfoundland. Wide-bodied aircraft could not be used to full capacity from Glasgow. Landing charges, they said, were four times higher at Prestwick than at Heathrow and three times higher than Glasgow — hardly an incentive to use the airport, and they questioned BAA's motive in the disposal of land around Prestwick through their property arm Lynton plc — land they claimed was worth £27million.

They tackled noise and pollution issues which were important to local residents. Glasgow flight paths were over built-up areas. The committee's submission was supported by hundreds of letters from companies, community councils and individuals. This was a hugely-important and stressful time, but it did have its lighter moments. Ian Welsh was in regular contact with George Younger and they had met early morning in a dark corner of Edinburgh Airport to discuss some final points at the start of the week when the government were going to come to a decision on Open Skies. The submission had been delivered and they were awaiting the result. Younger was an astute and experienced politician, but didn't seem to fully realise the tide was running against them. He was confident things were going to be okay.

Welsh recalls: "George said he would let me know as soon as he heard. Later that week I got a call at school, while I was in the middle of teaching what you might call a 'challenging' class of third-year pupils. A secretary looked in and said in hushed tones, 'There's a Mr Younger to speak to you.'

"George said, 'It's Open Skies. What do we do now?' And while one of the boys in my class decided to hang with one hand out of the second-floor window, much to the delight of his classmates who were shouting encouragement, the ex-Secretary of State for Scotland and Defence Secretary was asking me what we should do next to save Prestwick Airport! I told him we had to speak to British Aerospace."

Younger was to confirm later that Cecil King, head of British Airways, and BAA were very influential in putting pressure on the government and Margaret Thatcher for Open Skies to go ahead and, as Younger was coming to the end of his political career, his influence was not as pronounced as it might have been. Another man with Ayrshire connections also had the ear of Thatcher at this crucial time. David Campbell, who lives in Largs, was president of the powerful and influential Glasgow Chamber of Commerce during 1988-89. He also owned a number of Ayrshire weekly newspapers, including the *Ayr Advertiser* and *Troon And Prestwick Times* which, of course, were loudly campaigning for Prestwick. Wearing his Glasgow Chamber hat, he was fighting Glasgow's corner. He considered it vital for Scotland that the Open Skies policy be adopted. "I appreciate that living in Ayrshire, friends and neighbours might not necessarily see it that way with regards to Prestwick, but it was obvious to me at the time that BAA had no plans for Prestwick and airlines were voting with their feet and moving out. Prestwick was dying."

Campbell admits they were fighting some strong political lobbying from George Younger and Secretary of State Malcolm Rifkind, who was against Open Skies at the time. However, late in 1989, Campbell was a guest at a small exclusive political dinner with Margaret Thatcher in the College of Surgeons in Edin-

burgh, which was to prove a landmark in the Open Skies campaign. He said: "Mrs Thatcher had had rather a long day and after a couple of large whiskies she was in one of her moods and wanted to talk — you know, the 'ask me anything' kind of thing. So I said she was no doubt aware of the Open Skies issue and the importance to Scotland of opening this up from an economic and tourism point of view. The economy was heavily dependent on it, and so on. She said: 'Good point isn't it, Malcolm?' who went a bit red in the face as he was backing Prestwick.

"'I have been discussing this with Malcolm,' she said, 'and I think you will have an answer pretty soon.' After dinner, her private secretary took me aside

Concorde was a regular visitor to Prestwick in the 1980s and 1990s for pilot training
Photograph courtesy of Phil Toman

and said 'Don't worry, you've got it.' I looked at him. 'Open Skies,' he said. And that's how the first disclosure was made."

It wasn't until the following March that Transport Minister Cecil Parkinson formally announced the Open Skies policy for Scotland. It was felt by many that it was no coincidence that the announcement was timed for just after Younger announced he would be standing down at the next election. David Campbell to this day has no regrets about Open Skies. "I genuinely think it was in the best interests of Scotland, though not necessarily in the best interests of Ayrshire," he said. Others see it differently and there is still some bitterness that an Ayrshire man should have fought so hard in Glasgow's corner against Prestwick. He was given a rough ride when he was a guest at an Ayrshire Chamber of Commerce and Industry dinner held in the restaurant at Prestwick Airport shortly afterward, when he was openly booed. Sam Milliken, the Gateway Prestwick Action Committee convener who had fought so hard against Open Skies said: "He should never be forgiven for the damage he did to Ayrshire."

As soon as the skies opened, the deluge began and it looked as if Prestwick was spiralling on a tailspin to closure. The effects were immediate and catastrophic. Almost overnight, nine airlines announced their intention to fly transatlantic from Glasgow. There was a rush to see who could be first. These included the two remaining Prestwick scheduled airlines, Air Canada and Northwest. There were tears as the last Air Canada flight took off from Prestwick for Toronto on May 14, 1990. The airline had been flying from Ayrshire for almost 50 years

The commercial race was on in a big way. Northwest signalled its intention to start its Boston service out of Glasgow on May 1. They wanted to be "first out of Glasgow". In a double blow, Air Canada, not content with transferring its passenger flights to Halifax and Toronto, also announced it was thinking of moving its freight operations to Glasgow. British Airways and British Midland planned flights to New York and American Airlines announced a service to Chicago. Air 2000, the airline which started it all in 1983, was going to relaunch its direct Florida flights.

The Scottish Airports managing director at the time, Vernon Murphy, who had spearheaded the campaign for Open Skies, saw the move of the major transatlantic carriers to Glasgow as inevitable. They were, as he saw it, good for business and good for Scotland. "It was not an airport thing, it was an airline thing," he said, "and really came down to where the airlines wanted to fly from. That was really what it was all about." For years, he said, the major carriers had been telling him they wanted to fly out of Glasgow, not Prestwick.

While Glasgow's transatlantic service was booming, it was a different picture at Prestwick, where there were almost-deserted departure gates and runways. A report by analysts Nomura Research Institute bluntly concluded that as a result of Open Skies, passenger throughput at Prestwick would fall from 322,000 in 1989/90 to 60,000/90,000 in 1991 and that it was "entirely feasible that cargo alone will be handled in 1991/92".

In 1990 freight business was good at Prestwick. In fact the conditions and facilities for freight operations on which BAA appeared to be pinning their hopes for Prestwick's future were considered to be unparalleled in the UK. Cargo operators and manufacturers depended on them and business had doubled in four years to 18,000 tonnes. As congestion at other airports, notably London's, built up, Prestwick became increasingly attractive to businesses even in the south. As the year went on, however, confidence in even that side of the business began to

DAILY RECORD, Wednesday,

PRESTWICK HIT BY PULL-OUT SHOCKER

BA plan freight axe

THE FUTURE of Prestwick was under threat last night as British Airways got set to announce plans to AXE freight operations at the airport.

The proposed move will cut nearly TWO-THIRDS of the terminal's yearly freight business.

And last night pro-Prestwick campaign boss councillor Ian Welsh said: "This is becoming Ayrshire's Ravenscraig. It'll have a catastrophic effect on the local and the Scottish economies."

By IAIN FERGUSON and LACHIE KENNEDY

Airport bosses have already been told of BA's decision, which will effectively wipe Prestwick off the air freight map.

It follows the axing of the airport's trans-atlantic monopoly in Scotland. And the pull-out could happen as early as October 30.

BA said last night: "No

him freight was Prestwick's future.

He went on: "If he believes his own words, he must pressure BA to reverse the decision.

"If they go, others will follow and the knock-on affect will kill the airport."

GLOOM

English airports like Manchester.

"It'll have a disastrous affect. Other airines will pull out and there will be nothing left."

Prestwick general manager Ron Wallace was unavailable for comment last night.

The late 1980s and early 90s were nerve-wracking times for Prestwick... campaigners believed that the BAA was secretly preparing to shutdown the airport. Meanwhile, stories like this only exacerbated fears.

wane. In November, as Air Canada, still at Prestwick, increased its freight flights to three a week, British Airways were moving all of theirs to Glasgow. The same month saw talks with Fed-Ex about creating a freight hub at Prestwick fold. The plans for a Europe-based operation were badly affected by the increase in fuel costs at that time. It was not going their way, but the campaigners would not give in. As they saw it, they had lost a battle, not the war. The airport had such a long and glorious history they could not let it close. The problem was: how could they keep Prestwick flying?

Cecil Parkinson, following the Open Skies announcement, told BAA to bring landing charges at Prestwick in line with Glasgow and to cut freight costs to try to ensure a future for the airport. BAA were still promoting the official line: there were no plans for the closure of Prestwick, despite ominous signs that the opposite was true. Services began to haemorrhage, and surveyors were called in. It really began to look as if they were planning to close the airport despite all the denials. Eddie Clark, Kyle and Carrick District Council's estates manager who was still retained on an airport remit, said: "We couldn't believe what was happening. You don't just dispose of an airport. No other country in the world would think of getting rid of such an asset."

It was decided the Keep Prestwick Flying campaign should take a different tack. The council had considered the sale of the airport to be an option in safe-

guarding its future, but wasn't interest in buying the airport on its own. However, they decided they would be involved if anyone else expressed an interest in buying it. They saw it as a community asset and one they had to keep.

Two months after Open Skies, efforts were still going on to attract new passengers to Prestwick. Talks were held with Emerald Air in an effort to start a daily service to London, with links to Northern Ireland and the continent. There was also a planned tie-up with Eagle Air to allow flights to Reykjavic in Iceland, which could have transatlantic connections. George Younger made an announcement about the planned service in May 1990 and said they would be using Jetstream 31s — being produced at the neighbouring British Aerospace plant. Unfortunately, the plans did not materialise. Then, in a further disappointment, the government rejected a proposal that had been put forward for a Prestwick rail halt. Transport Minister, Lord James Douglas Hamilton, said it would be too

When it's foggy in Glasgow, it's always clear and, therefore, busy at Prestwick
Photograph courtesy of Phil Toman

expensive, particularly bearing in mind the decrease in passengers now using the airport. And if you're thinking the name sounds familiar, the then Transport Minister is the youngest son of the 14th Duke Of Hamilton, co-founder of Scottish Aviation with David McIntyre! He later went on to write a book about his father's meeting with Rudoph Hess.

Arguments that the rail stop could help attract new passengers also fell on deaf ears. On the day the rail halt proposal was thrown out, a cross-party group of MPs and councillors met with Sir Norman Payne, chairman of BAA, to express their growing fears for the airport's future, but they got little reassurance. In a move to get transatlantic charters to go from Prestwick in place of the removed scheduled services, Ian Welsh prepared a five-point plan for Scottish Secretary Malcolm Rifkind, asking for government intervention to halt the airport's decline. Deaf ears again

At the airport, meantime, supporters could see no obvious signs of efforts being made by BAA to replace the lost transatlantic business. While the campaigners were drawing up plans and frantically looking for ways to keep Prestwick flying, the immediate effect of Open Skies was felt by the workforce. One hundred jobs went immediately following the announcement and there was worse to come. Various airport services started to be cut back. By April, scarcely a month on, a courtesy coach to take passengers on the five-minute journey from the airport to the railway station in Prestwick town centre had been withdrawn and there was growing evidence that BAA were actively discouraging new flights into the airport. The same month, the status of the fire and rescue service was reduced to Category 7, which meant that the airport would no longer be able to accept 747 Jumbo jets and it was planned to reduce it further by the October which meant the airport would not be able to accept Tri-stars, DC10s or 757s. Pilots would no longer be able to list Prestwick as a diversionary airfield when logging a flight plan, this in spite of its good weather record. October was starting to look ominous, a key date in BAA's calendar for major change, perhaps even closure. The terminal porters were given notice to quit, to take effect from the October and the contract cleaners were given six months notice — there would be no cleaning service after October. The various car-hire operators and other franchise holders were told that BAA were prepared to enter into negotiations for the termination of their franchises, also from October. Duty-free operators were in the same position.

Sam Milliken wrote to Sir John Egan, chief executive of BAA, on behalf of the Gateway Action Committee to voice their concern that passenger and cargo operators and concessionaires were being fobbed off when they asked about the availability of the airport for passenger flights the following year. Morale amongst staff was low and would be made worse the following October, when a further 60 jobs would be axed, almost half the remaining workforce. The supporters were in no doubt: Prestwick Airport was being run down in preparation for closure.

The general manager in charge of running down the various services was Lesley Bale, and Prestwick campaigners were convinced she had been brought in to close it down completely. Paddy Healy, later to become managing director of the airport but at that time commanding officer of the neighbouring navy search and rescue base, HMS Gannet, remembers Bale calling him and telling him she was going to remove the air traffic control services from Prestwick. "What are you going to do?" she asked. "I'll tell you what I'm going to do," Healy told her. "I will land all the Sea King helicopters in the field beside the airport and there's nothing you can do about it. You can't stop me flying. I'll take off without permission, but you will have a real problem when I tell the newspapers that you have removed

Search-and-Rescue from the west coast of Scotland to the Isle of Man."

Healey asked her: "Have you told your boss yet what you plan to do? I suggest you do." Bale was back within an hour to say: "Forget it."

Despite all the evidence on the ground, Scottish Airports boss Vernon Murphy maintains to this day that to his knowledge, complete closure was NOT on BAA's agenda for Prestwick. They could not keep on running the airport at full capacity, as it was losing too much money, was not attracting new airlines and had virtually no passengers. Despite that, he maintains he was not aware of plans to close it down totally, though he does concede that mothballing the airport was an option. This would have involved keeping the country's only long-haul runway working on a care-and-maintenance basis for British Aerospace, the neighbouring flying school, and HMS Gannet. BAA, said Murphy, were doing all they could to try to keep it going. "Everything was tried to attract new business to the airport throughout the 1980s, but these had failed. They included sales missions to the US and Canada to encourage North American tourism and the offer of cut-rate charges to European traffic to attract charter flights. They all failed." Most of these initiatives to boost Prestwick were not made public at the time, he said, to avoid more bad publicity.

Mothballing. Closure. The Prestwick supporters were not prepared to consider either option. By this time they knew the only way they could save the airport was by persuading BAA to sell it — but to whom, and who was going to do the persuading?

What they did not realise was that behind the scenes, quietly and deliberately, plans were already being laid to do just that.

Chapter 4
The Talented
Mr Hudson

O N A WET afternoon in the late summer of 1990, retired Canadian lawyer, entrepreneur and millionaire Matthew Hudson was sitting in his study looking at plans he was drawing up for a nine-hole golf course he wanted to build around his home overlooking the village of Kirkoswald in rural South Ayrshire. He had moved into Blanefield House the previous year with his family. It was a large country pile built in 1900 by Sir Gilbert Blane, the man responsible for the world-famous Turnberry Hotel, and was formerly owned by the Marques and Marchioness of Ailsa. The phone rang and the voice at the other end was that of Ayr MP George Younger, who introduced himself and said to Hudson: "Have you heard about Prestwick Airport?" Hudson said he knew it only as the place where he met his mother when she came on holiday from Canada.

"I have been fighting to save it for years," said Younger, "And I think you might be the man who can help me save it for Ayrshire and for Scotland."

Younger's desperation had been increasing since Cecil Parkinson had announced Open Skies. The future of Prestwick Airport looked bleak, services were in the process of being run down, business was haemorrhaging, and closure was a very distinct possibility. There were various schemes in the pipeline — like the proposed link-up with Emerald Airways, but Younger knew the only real hope for the airport was to persuade BAA to sell. Plus, he was about to stand down and he didn't want to be remembered as the MP who oversaw the closure of Prestwick. He had to save the airport and he had to find the right man to help him do it. It wasn't just the future of the airport and its workers that was at stake, though that was bad enough. Younger realised that closure of the airport put the future of the British Aerospace factory and its large workforce in jeopardy.

Here the campaigners had struck lucky. The general manager at British Aerospace Prestwick, at the time, was Allan MacDonald, Ayr born-and-bred and a Scot through and through with a passion for his local airport. Things could have turned out so differently had the man in charge not had such local loyalties. According to MacDonald, the Prestwick plant had been on BAe's hit-list for years. "I had to fight every year to keep it alive," he said. "We had no major aircraft programmes, we weren't making money, the airport and runway weren't ours. We didn't own the site. We were constantly on the BAe closure list and George Younger and I had to fight really hard to keep it alive."

BAe at Prestwick, along with Shorts of Belfast, had been scheduled for closure under the Labour Government's Nationalisation Act of 1977, but pressure from Younger along with Ayrshire Labour MPs persuaded the government, at the very last minute, to keep the plant open. However its future was constantly on the line

Previous page: Canadian entrepreneur Matthew Hudson was designing a golf course for his home when George Younger called and asked him to spearhead the fight to save Prestwick *Photo courtesy of Mirrorpix*

and it was not considered a major player in the aerospace industry as far as the business leaders were concerned. "We were like an irritating pimple to them. But to George Younger and myself, we were talking about 3,000 jobs at that time," said MacDonald. He was lucky in that he had become friends with the company chief executive, Sir Dick Evans, when they both began their careers with BAe. Their friendship continued over the years and part of MacDonald's strategy in keeping the Prestwick plant secure was to woo the company chief executive with the attraction of a game of golf at the world-famous Old Prestwick course, home of the first Open Golf Championship, during his regular visits to the plant. Along with Younger he shrewdly engineered things so that Sir Dick became a member of the exclusive golf club where BAe had corporate membership. MacDonald was convinced this helped whenever the future of Prestwick was being discussed at high level. Sir Dick, he believed, developed a fondness for the plant and its workforce on his regular visits and this helped keep it off the closure list. "When it comes to dishing out credit for the saving of Prestwick Airport I think Prestwick Golf Course should be high on the list," said MacDonald, remembering the many "meetings" carried out on the course.

When BAA plc first started rationalising and made Glasgow their centre of operations, MacDonald recognised it wasn't just the airport that was under threat, but the BAe plant itself. At the time they were manufacturing the highly-successful Jetstream 31, a 19-seater turbo prop aircraft aimed mainly at the American commuter market. Suddenly, he could see a nightmare scenario developing before his eyes: BAA selling Prestwick to a company not interested in keeping it as an airport, who would close it, demolish the terminal and develop the property, including the runway, maybe with houses, giving BAe the perfect excuse for closure of his factory: no airport, no runway, no aircraft plant. Production would be moved south of the border and it wouldn't be their fault. BAe could put its hands in the air laying the blame at BAA's door. To MacDonald, this was a disaster waiting to happen. He had been working in England and Saudi Arabia; he had worked on the Lightning and Strikemaster programmes, then had come back home to commercial aircraft and Prestwick and he wasn't prepared to give up his plant without a fight. He was only too happy to work with George Younger on a plan to save both – the commercial airport and the aircraft plant.

Younger, meantime, realising the only way the airport could survive was under new owners, was looking round for the right man to head up a buy-out. He knew he had local businessmen already interested in saving the airport, particularly Bill Miller, but they needed the right man to head up and plan such a deal. Allan MacDonald had met Matthew Hudson at Farnborough Air Show in 1990. Hudson was living near Bath and had saved a small aircraft company in England from foreclosure. Although small, the company was the only non-BAe entity left in the UK producing a CAA-certificated aircraft of its own, the Optica. Hudson had then expanded its portfolio into sub-contract work for BAe. The Optica was being featured at Farnborough that year, being flown by Neville Duke.

As part of his purchase of the company, Hudson had also acquired control of Old Sarum Airfield, next to Farnborough, the oldest continually-licensed airfield in the UK. When they met, MacDonald was impressed with Hudson's entrepreneurial skills and his declared commitment to support British aviation in any way he could. MacDonald shared his enthusiasm with George Younger — and the game was on.

Younger discovered Hudson was a man with a wide range of business and entrepreneurial skills. Born in Ontario, Canada, in 1942, Hudson attended Queens University, graduating with a first-class law degree, while also honing his business skills. He owned and operated a landscaping and garden business then, while an articled clerk, he set up his own printing and advertising business. Following graduation from Osgoode Hall and qualification as a barrister and solicitor in 1969, he took up a challenge as a Company Doctor (CEO) for a subsidiary of ITT in Montreal. He was then headhunted in the early 1970s by Cadillac Development Corporation, which propelled him into the world of property development. By the late 1970s he had gone into property development on his own account in Montreal, moving late, and very successfully, into property development, oil and gas exploration and electronics in the USA.

By the mid-1980s, a multi-millionaire, two marriages behind him and with five children, Hudson decided it was time for a change of scene and moved from his base in New Jersey across the Atlantic to the UK with his four daughters, Genevieve, 10, Alexandra, eight, Rebecca, seven and Meredith, three. Travelling with them was their English nanny, Pamela Forsyth, later to become the third Mrs Hudson. They moved into an estate home near Bath. His son Mark, then 20, remained in Canada. "Business had become stale in the US," said Hudson. "I was involved in various types of venture capital. I was always the venturer and it was almost always my capital. It is not all that challenging once you learn how to do hotels, apartment buildings, shopping centres, golf courses. I ran out of new things to do. Then a low-carbon ferrochrome project caught my attention and fitted a UK location."

While still in the States he had become a principal investor with, and then a good friend of, Sir Monty Finniston, former chairman of British Steel. With Sir Monty and building magnate Lord Edwin McAlpine, Hudson planned to build a low-arbon ferrochrome plant on the River Clyde in Scotland. The project fell through, said Hudson, when the inventor reneged and threw in his lot with a penny stock company on the Vancouver Exchange. Hudson then moved into the aerospace investment business, meeting the Friday payroll for a small Wiltshire aircraft manufacturer as the result of a Thursday phone call while on holiday with his family in Cannes at Easter 1986. He renamed the company Brooklands Aerospace and invited Alan Curtis, the former chairman of Lotus, to chair the company.

Brooklands Aerospace had developed the Optica, a bubble-fronted small aircraft designed as a surveillance tool, specially suited for the police, military and other NGOs. Under Hudson's leadership and investment, the Optica gained FAA

As a well-connected, successful Scottish businessman, Bill Miller was a natural choice to join the PIK board
Published with permission of Bill Miller

certification and he negotiated the removal of the manufacturing to Utva in Yugoslavia to permit lower pricing to enable large numbers of sales. After the second Optica sent to the States was ruined onboard the ship at sea, Lloyds Bank obtained personal guarantees from Hudson and Curtis and then quickly withdrew its support, forcing the company into the hands of the Receivers.

In late 1985, Hudson had met Sir David McNee, former Strathclyde Police Chief Constable and Commissioner of London's Metropolitan Police, for discussions and advice before starting up his own security company and the two became close friends. Sir David went on to become a director of Control Technology, a company that Hudson had formed several years earlier to pursue his ideas in remote measurement and monitoring. In 1988, Hudson married Pamela Forsyth and Sir David gave the bride away at the ceremony in a small village church outside Bath where the Optica "danced" over the garden in the hands of Neville Duke.

Later that year they moved to Ayrshire, setting up home at Blanefield. Hudson had been considering a move to the Channel Islands, but his three Scottish friends, Sir Monty Finniston, Lord Edwin McAlpine and Sir David McNee, along with Pamela (whose grandad was a Glasgow man) persuaded him to set his sights on Scotland. Considering himself semi-retired, he began restoring his new home to its former grandeur but with the addition of modern features, resetting the hundreds of windows and carrying out extensive garden works. Once the house and gardens were completed, by the end of 1989, he turned his attention to the estate and decided he wanted to create his own nine-hole golf course. It was at this point the phone rang.

"George told me on the phone who he was — I had never met him," said Hudson. "He said he had been fighting for Prestwick Airport for so long and had almost given up hope. He said he hoped I was the man who could help him save the airport. George was at his wits end at that time. He had tried everything and he knew that BAA had plans to mothball or close the airport. I later joked with him that it was a mark of his desperation that he called me. In fact I heard from my own doctor in Ayr not long after this phone call that he had had one of the BAA chaps in who told him they had bids in for the demolition of the terminal. That's how close it was to closure. It was very rainy that day, and I wasn't ready to start building my golf course, so I said: 'I'll take a look at it for you George,' thinking it would take me two or three weeks. My first thought was: *should* the airport be saved? Then I asked myself: why are airports important?"

Hudson began to research the operation of major airports and their economic influence. After three weeks he was able to report some progress. He was no further along in terms of saving it, but he had now convinced himself that it needed to be saved, not only for Ayrshire but for the Scottish economy. He decided to work on it some more. He had to learn about aviation, navigation, route drivers and then how it could all fit in. He had to learn who and what were the drivers in the Scottish economy, with the electronics industry at the top of the list. He dedicated himself to learning about electronics and Just in Time manufacturing, which was beginning to become important. He turned to Bill Miller, who lived in the neighbouring town of Maybole. Miller, had already been heavily involved in discussions with George Younger concerning the future of the airport. "He had been in the hi-tech industry and as Airport Consultative Committee chairman had been deeply involved in the campaign to save the airport," said Hudson. "He was the ideal person to set up meetings with the MDs of the major electronics companies." And he did. Miller was instrumental in helping him understand the logistics driving PC manufacture and assembly. That was key to the first main plank of saving the airport. Freight.

"We needed a plan to develop a capability to handle an existing, coalesced and recognized need. That was freight as I came to imagine it. Passengers were very much Phase 2," he said. "As I said many times in many places in Scotland in the early days, freight is what your airport does for your industries, incoming passengers is what your airport does for your tourism-based industries and you going to London and the continent and the States — that is what you are doing for those places."

It was obvious to Hudson that the way BAA operated Prestwick Airport was unsustainable; they were spending two pounds for each pound of revenue. He needed to invent a new business model, and began by learning about how large airports were operated. He read all the UK rules and regulations; CAA regulations, how they operated; all about the Crash Rescue Service; air traffic control. This went on for a number of months throughout 1990 as the services were being run down at the airport. After steeping himself in how airports operated, he came up with a new business model: instead of concessioning everything out, you did everything with your own staff. There was no down time; everybody worked a full shift, including the fire fighters of the Crash Rescue Service. Everyone would need at least two skills — a revenue skill and a safety skill. This was unheard of at that time. He put together this business model and met with Younger in Edinburgh at the Royal Bank where he had become chairman. Hudson told him: "Okay. Yes, it should be saved.

This is why it is important to Scotland. Here's how it can become part of the Scottish economic engine and here's how it needs to work operationally to allow it to be lean and keen and do the right job and be able to make money. Here's a business model, an operating model and a strategic five-year marketing plan, a nice little package. I've done what you asked me to do. All you have to do is go and find some investors."

Hudson recalled: "He said to me, 'Nobody will invest in this. This is Scotland. Everybody knows BAA is the world's best operator. They run Aberdeen, Glasgow, Edinburgh, Heathrow, Gatwick, Stansted. They've said this airport's no good; that there's no market to support it; that it's too expensive to operate. I know what you've done is marvellous but nobody will take it on. Will you do it?'

"I said: 'George, I have a nine-hole golf course to build. Let me think about it.'"

So Hudson drove home and thought about it and then called back Younger and said: "I don't know if I can do it all, but I will try on two conditions: most importantly you must agree to be chairman of the board of any group that is set up and secondly, I want to stay retired so I won't operate the airport myself. I will be on the board as your deputy, but someone else will need to run it."

With agreement reached, the next problem was how to get the airport out of BAA's hands.

By the end of 1990 BAA were really beginning to feel the pressure. What were they going to do with Prestwick Airport? Glasgow was now the centre of their Scottish operations, Prestwick was superfluous to their needs and they wanted to eliminate it as a commercial challenge to Glasgow. With hindsight, it seems incredible a company should be thinking of closing an airport, but in the commercial climate of 1990 BAA wanted to rid themselves of Prestwick. Rightly or wrongly, they saw it as too remote and a financial drain as it was losing more than £2 million a year. But it did have wonderful property value and BAA had recently acquired Lynton Properties, a property development subsidiary, in a high-profile transaction.

It could be they planned to keep a portion of the main runway open in the short term on a care-and-maintenance basis for British Aerospace and its flying school, as Vernon Murphy said, but that left plenty of room for other development opportunities on the surrounding land. The terminal could be demolished and they could use their property development subsidiary to recycle the airport ground at a huge profit, though there was one flaw in that plan: it was becoming obvious to BAA that George Younger was not going away, nor were his vociferous band of supporters in Ayrshire. It was also becoming increasingly clear they were going to have to consider selling the airport. Younger was still a considerable political force to be reckoned with, even though he was by now out of the cabinet and was standing down at the next election. He was chairman of the Royal Bank of Scotland and still had the ear of Margaret Thatcher — he was her election campaign manager. Furthermore, he had something to prove. He did not want his political legacy to be a closed airport and the consequent unemployment disaster. Younger understood full well that

Prestwick had Scotland's only long-haul runway and, based on Matthew Hudson's work, he knew the full economic implications of using that runway correctly.

There was also growing political support for the sale of Prestwick from Labour. John Prescott, then Shadow Transport Secretary, who had addressed the airport workers in 1990, told representatives of the aviation industry at a meeting in London that he was totally unimpressed by the results of the Open Skies policy and the effect it had had on Prestwick. He told the audience, which included BAA chairman Sir Norman Payne and Lord King of British Airways, that while Labour did not have plans to re-nationalise airports he thought there should be increased local involvement in the running of them. He wanted to see the private and public sector working towards a properly-integrated transport system in the UK. "Something must be done about Prestwick," he said. "I hope it does not end up as a supermarket."

A spokesman for the Scottish Airports, replying to Prescott's comments, said the airport was not for sale. However, he added that Scottish Airports would listen to any sensible offer or proposal. He said: "We have heard much of consortia waiting in the wings with millions of pounds at their disposal, but so far no one has come up with any firm proposal." That, however, was about to change. By early 1991, while Hudson was fine-tuning his development plan for Younger, potential

buyers were beginning to emerge, circling like vultures round a kill. It may have been dying, but various groups saw potential in the carcass, rich pickings for some. First away from the blocks in declaring an interest at this time were property developer Peter Kaye, from Millport on the Isle of Cumbrae, and business partner Gordon Watson. Kaye owned Channel Islands Airways and a glass company. Watson had been a technical director with Scottish Aviation at Prestwick and had gone on to become BAA's General Manager of Airports in Scotland in the early 1980s. A freight company and some unnamed businessmen were said to be backing their bid. They called themselves AAP.

Also interested was Bill Barr, who, in addition to being a nationally-known builder, head of Barr Ltd, was chairman of the local football club Ayr United. Barr was also chairman of the board operating the Freeport at the airport. The Freeport had been set up on land given over by BAA in 1984 in an effort to "boost business" at the airport, though it had never been fully developed. Prestwick supporters at the time saw this gift as one of the early signs of asset-stripping by BAA in the lead-up to their planned closure of the airport, as the land included much of the second runway which BAA subsequently closed and leased to a sheep farmer. Allan Mac-

A USAF C-17 Globemaster, left, a regular arrival on Prestwick's long runway; and above, the eccentrically-shaped Airbus A300B *Photographs courtesy of dtownsend@wightcablenorth.net*

Donald, mindful of BAe's, future also lodged his company's interest in any planned purchase.

George Younger, meantime, in his position as local MP, was being approached by the various potential buyers and he decided it would be best if the various groups could come together rather than have them become involved in a competitive battle for BAA's favour. At Younger's request, Matthew Hudson arranged to meet with Peter Kaye and Gordon Watson at his home in March 1991. He invited Bill Miller to join the meeting and draft terms for a Heads of Agreement were proposed. The proposal set out that the two sides would work together to buy the airport and run it as a going concern while looking at opportunities for related leisure-based developments. However, in detailing their plans, Peter Kaye and Gordon Watson proposed a two-company structure — one to operate the airfield and the other to pursue the potential of leisure activities. It also became clear during the talks that while they said they wanted to keep the airport open, Kaye and Watson didn't rule out developing the whole site.

BAe were obviously going to be a major player with whoever was going to take over the airport, so Allan MacDonald also met with Kaye and Watson and he appreciated early on that Kaye saw the airport as an area ripe for development and he sensed he had no real interest in keeping it open. Watson, he felt, was in the partnership to lend credibility with the community and workforce because of his BAA experience, but as he wasn't putting any money into the deal, he was merely a figurehead and held little sway with Kaye. It also quickly became apparent to Mac-Donald that one of the early consequences of a buyout involving Kaye and Watson would be the complete closure of the second runway, as Kaye wanted to recoup his investment right away by building quality houses on the site. Alarm bells started to ring since the second runway was critical to BAe's flight operations. The Jetstream 31 and the bigger 41 were both being manufactured by this time and BAe had to demonstrate to potential buyers that they could land in all wind conditions. For that, they needed access to the second runway. There was also the neighbouring BAe flying college to be considered; it might also go out of business if the second runway was closed.

MacDonald realised the result of a Kaye/Watson buyout could play into the hands of both BAe and BAA. It would lead to the total closure of the airport, which he believed was what some at BAe head office wanted. MacDonald said: "Soon after I saw them, George and I met and agreed we could not support a Kaye/Watson buyout of the airport for it would undoubtedly have led to the withdrawal of BAe from Prestwick for 'legal technical reasons' [i.e. no second runway] and that would have meant the loss of thousands of jobs."

D-Day for this joint proposal was April 5, when there was a showdown in Mac-Donald's office which resulted in Kaye and Watson walking out. MacDonald told the meeting he did not like the two-company structure proposed in the draft Heads of Agreement and that BAe was not prepared to join any such consortium. Kaye

Kyle and Carrick District Council's Ian Welsh cultivated a strong grass-roots campaign to save the airport

and Watson were not happy with the 25 per cent share in the consortium they were being offered and turned it down, not wanting to be in a "subservient position". An exchange of angry letters followed, and despite his diplomatic skills, George Younger could not pour oil on these troubled waters and the end result was the break-up of any plan to work together.

The Younger-inspired group of local business-men, headed by Hudson, then began to take shape. Hudson's purpose in putting a group together was not financially-motivated — indeed he agreed to put up the risk funds needed to bankroll all the preliminary work and to underwrite the purchase of the airport. His shared purpose with Younger was to mutually choose what he described as "well-known patriots of impeccable integrity" who had the skills to operate closely as colleagues in a high-profile, high-risk Scottish venture — in other words his own team. Hudson had chosen a title for his band of businessmen — the Ayrshire Community Airport Project — a name carefully selected to show they had the best interests of the community at heart.

Bill Miller was the first recruit to the group, a natural choice because of his experience as the founder of the first Scottish public circuit board manufacturer and his long history of public support for the airport. Then came Jim Moffat and his wife Margie. Moffat was the founder and former head of AT Mays, the Ayrshire travel agent group which, at its peak, had 300 branches throughout the UK. His experience in the travel industry would prove invaluable if their bid was success-ful. Moffat loved Prestwick Airport. The group was later joined by Tim Morrison, non-executive director of Morrison Bowmore Distillers, a member of the R&A and shortly thereafter owner of John Letters, the Scottish golf club manufacturer. He was also a local fine wine merchant and, along with his wife Maggie, close friends of Matthew and Pamela Hudson. "It must be said he joined ACAP against the advice of Adam Bank, then his financial advisors, but he was prepared to take the risk," said Hudson.

At this early stage, this group of high-profile Ayrshire businessmen agreed to commit £50,000 each towards the airport buyout. Younger, because of his political position, was exempted from this agreement. These funds were placed in a separate account by Hudson and in fact were never used for funding purposes. He felt "it was enough these men were risking their reputations without risking their coin".

They would be joined later by Sir David McNee. His contribution, Hudson thought, would be invaluable for his uncommon common sense, his insights into the Scottish character and his first-hand knowledge as to how HMG dealt with matters Scottish. Each of these very successful Scots was aware they were staking not just cash but their considerable reputations on a potential deal which was not being taken seriously by the business community. "You're buying what?" was the general response when any of the group members brought up the subject at social gatherings.

Peter Kaye and Gordon Watson, meantime, did not disappear from the scene. They decided to lobby BAA and became the favoured buyers with the company's top brass in London.

Bill Barr was still interested in joining up with any consortium planning to buy the airport and in May 1991 ACAP met with him, leading to plans for a joint venture which would also involve another Ayrshire man, Scott Grier, boss of the successful airline Loganair. It was agreed that 10 per cent of any deal agreed would go to a selected merchant bank and 30 per cent was to be offered to BAe. Younger was confirmed non-executive chairman and Hudson the executive deputy chairman. The other directors would be Miller, Moffat, Barr and, following the appropriate acceptances, Grier and MacDonald. It looked good on paper, but this proposed consortium was also to receive a setback when Barr revised his views on the arrangements and indicated his disagreement with the terms at the outset of the first meeting. He left, and the meeting continued without him. Scott Grier also withdrew from the consortium, due to his other business commitments.

Having done the bidding of their chairman, by talking to other interested parties, ACAP was happy to be standing alone again and by midsummer the pace was hotting up. By August 1991, matters were coming to a head. It had been recognised early on by Hudson and MacDonald that it would be smart for ACAP and BAe to worke closely together on a buyout, since research into the history of the airport revealed that no buyer would have unfettered title to the airport without the necessary consents and releases from BAe. This dated back to the deal hammered out between Scottish Aviation and David MacIntyre and the government.

Both men agreed they could make a powerful team. BAe had the history, not to mention the clout, and ACAP had the backing of the community and, they hoped, the council. As part of his strategy, Hudson had been speaking to Kyle and Carrick District Council. He knew he had to get them on his side since, after all, a property and leisure development, as put forward by BAA and Kaye/Watson, could have sounded very attractive to the council. Hudson spoke to Councillor Welsh, the veteran campaigner for the airport. They met in the Provost's room in Ayr Town Hall and Welsh admits he had strong reservations at first. Who was this Canadian carpetbagger? Who was *he* to muscle in on the scene? What did he know about the airport? But Younger had recommended him, so Welsh was ready to give him the benefit of the doubt.

"Mind you I counted my fingers after we shook hands," laughed Welsh.

Hudson admits it must have been difficult for the local councillor. By this time other groups were showing their hand and talking to the council. "But I had the ace card," said Hudson. "I had George Younger's commitment to back me. Other groups may have claimed to have the support of Mr Younger, but as I said to Ian, 'If you want to know who he's really backing, that's easy — lift the phone and ask him.'

"We were lucky, Ian recognised redevelopment could be good for Ayrshire, but as a local leader who is an intelligent Scot he understood the need for it to be 'Scotland's Airport' and not a posh property development. He knew if they were putting together a consortium of prominent Scots who would risk their reputations, they had to make sure the council backed their plans, but they also had to find a way to make BAA sell to them and nobody else, because the property people were probably prepared to offer a lot more money."

In August, the personal agreement between Hudson and MacDonald was formalised, stating that ACAP and BAe would work on a joint bid. Approval from the main BAe board for the joint venture was expected in September. Meanwhile, at BAA's London headquarters, it seemed the ACAP bid was not being taken seriously. Hudson was really having to push the finance director of Scottish Airports, JP Sugden, to receive copies of information passed to other bidders for the airport. This was not helped by the fact there was no official prospectus of the airport for bidders and no definitive bundle of documents. It was also becoming clearer by the day that BAA were favouring the Peter Kaye and Gordon Watson bid after all. They seemed to want rid of any potential for competition for Glasgow in the west of Scotland and this made Kaye/Watson the natural front-runners as keeping the airport operating was not their top priority.

Younger and Hudson had plans to make the airport viable, but it was not *their* airport. How were they to prise the airport away from BAA and how could they persuade them to sell the airport to a competitor who would want to establish the airport's commercial viability at the expense of the BAA airports at Glasgow and Edinburgh? Not an easy task. It was time to pull out the ace card: the MacIntyre factor.

PIK

Chapter 5
The Mac
Factor

WHILE meetings had been going on throughout the spring and early summer of 1991 to create one consortium to put together a bid for the airport, one that would have the future of the airport and its workers at heart, Matthew Hudson had been following another trail. He initially was working on the premise that BAA had no intention of selling the airport. He was sure they were just humouring potential buyers and planned to develop it themselves through their property arm, Lynton Properties, which, following privatisation of BAA, had snapped up valuable land around the airport. He could see them turning it into a golf course with luxury housing and shops. Hudson said: "The airport was on the edge of the internationally-known Royal Troon and Prestwick golf courses, championship courses. In fact, Prestwick was the first course to stage The Open, the world's oldest golf championship. There was clearly enormous potential. Unlike much of the land about the airport, this land was structurally sound; it could support the largest aircraft in the world, fully laden and was ideal for building. They could also easily have had an 18-hole golf course with luxury housing and they would have made a lot of money, no question of that. BAA took the view that if they, the most successful airport operators in the world, could not make a success of Prestwick, no one could. But they saw no reason to turn down a massive windfall property profit."

The task was to find a way to persuade BAA to sell, and to sell to a group that wanted to continue operating it as a commercial airport, and that meant ACAP. It was not going to be easy, but Hudson was a man with a mission and, as ever, he had a plan. His close reading of Prestwick's history over the previous months had made him a staunch admirer of David McIntyre; one entrepreneur admiring the fortitude of another, one the original champion of Prestwick, the other an aspiring successor. He realised that the government had "taken" McIntyre's Prestwick Airport property from his company Scottish Aviation (SAL) initially for the purposes of WWII and that McIntyre had objected informally, formally and legally to the Government's actions. Hudson had read all the old Scottish Aviation documents that his ally Allan MacDonald could provide him with and based on that reading he felt that there must be one important document missing. He could see its footprint in the documents in the company archives, but the important document was not there.

By early summer, Hudson and Allan MacDonald had agreed it was in their mutual interest to work together on a deal to buy the entire site: airport, factory and runway, then they would split the assets, ACAP having the airport and BAe the factory site. Who would own the runway still had to be agreed at this stage. But they still had to convince the top brass of BAe and BAA that this was the way to go. Now the pair decided to join forces to look back at the historic agreement. Hudson didn't have the

Previous page: David Mcintyre standing outside the first training school building at Prestwick aerodrome in 1936 *Photograph courtesy of the David F. McIntyre Collection*

resources to carry out the search for the relevant documents, but BAe did. Working for BAe Prestwick at the time as company secretary was a young lawyer from Aberdeen, Jonathan Walton, who went on to be executive vice president of BAe in South Africa. MacDonald assigned Walton to work with Hudson on the search.

Walton, who had joined BAe in February 1991, was thus thrust into the battle for the airport. He said: "We felt that if BAA plc were prepared to sell Prestwick, it meant they had buyers already lined up — Peter Kaye and Gordon Watson. They had declared their intent to continue to operate the airport as such, but no one was sure about their long-term ability to run the airport or indeed their real intentions. There was a worry that they could sooner or later sell the airport land on to a property developer, who would cease airport operations and sell off the land, including the runway. I think Safeway were mentioned at the time as waiting in the wings and we believed BAA were keen and ready to do a deal with this buyer.

"Allan had this perception that BAe's use of the runway was somehow guaranteed in the 1953 deal between the government and David McIntyre but we were not sure how. The lease of the land on which the Prestwick factory was built did not explicitly guarantee BAe's use of the runway or indeed the continued existence of it."

They soon realised the only way to secure the runway for BAe's continued use was for BAe to own it, which meant they had to persuade BAA to sell to them. However, BAe did not want to run an airport; they would continue to operate the factory and perhaps even the runway, if necessary, but not the airport itself. In fact, Allan MacDonald considered it was imperative that it did not get out that BAe were even in talks to buy an airport, which would not have gone down well with the shareholders, he felt. MacDonald therefore chose instead to team up with ACAP. Both MacDonald and Hudson agreed the history of the airport held the key. There was something in the old records that guaranteed some rights to the site because of the nature of the compulsory purchase after the war. It was a question of finding it.

"My job, as instructed by Allan," said Walton, "was to find a legal basis for compelling BAA to drop their preferred buyer and negotiate exclusively with us with a view to securing a legal title to the Prestwick factory site plus the runway."

In the early summer of 1991, the two lawyers, the 49-year-old Canadian and the young Scot, began digging. Hudson provided Walton with a memo outlining his theory concerning the existence and likely contents of the mystery "missing" document.

Hudson's research had uncovered that there had been arbitration at some point in 1953, which may have settled the terms of a long-term use agreement in favour of SAL. He believed that within these proceedings lay an agreement or possibly a contract which guaranteed SAL's (now BAe's) use of the runway through the government, now represented by BAA. This deal would, he believed, establish BAe's legal right to continued use of the runway. Such a contract could be used to enforce BAA to either keep the runway open until the end of the term agreed in the negotiations or alternatively deal with BAe in the sale of Prestwick Airport land. It would also mean that BAA, as successor to the British Government as owners of the site, would be unable to pass on the burden of the guarantee to anyone else, such as Peter Kaye and Gordon Watson without the consent of BAe.

Hudson said: "The argument would be that there was simply no person or entity that would be capable of stepping into the shoes of a successor to the government as far as sustaining the guarantee of access to the runway was concerned. This would leave BAA with the unattractive prospect of being stuck with the airport, or, of course, selling it to BAe."

Now all Walton and Hudson had to do was *find* this elusive document. After extensive searches and several trips to government archives in London and elsewhere, Walton found a reference in the files which indicated that the clerk to the arbitrator in 1953 was an Edinburgh solicitor named Connell. Walton had joined BAe from an Edinburgh firm of solicitors and was familiar with a firm in the city called Connell and Connell. Bingo! The Connell referred to was indeed one of the firm's founder partners and a search in the archives uncovered the papers relating to the arbitration. Hudson and Walton searched a box of dusty old documents and discovered that the arbitration was in fact over the compulsory purchase of the Prestwick Airport site, including the business area, then dedicated to flying training.

The government's point in the argument was that during the war the War Ministry had transformed the airport from a simple aerodrome with no tarmac runway, ramps or taxiways to a fully-functioning military airport, and they wanted public ownership of the site as they had spent so much taxpayers' money modernising it. It was plain from the papers in the archive that Scottish Aviation intended to continue the business of flying training with plans to move into plane manufacturing, and both activities clearly needed a runway. The obvious and unambiguous intention of all parties at the time of the negotiations was for Scottish Aviation not to be prejudiced by its loss of ownership of the site and to continue and to develop its business with unlimited use of the runway — with a 99-year lease — while the airport was being developed separately.

"However," said Walton, "unfortunately the documents didn't quite spell that out. Under Scots law the arbitration documents on the face of it did not quite give us the clear 'contract' that we needed as a lever in our dealings with BAA. This is a technical legal issue, but the law would presume that the parties wrote down what they intended in a contract at the time. In this case that meant the 99-year lease."

With their new understanding of what the government and Scottish Aviation really meant to do, Hudson and Walton then went to work earnestly on the lease itself. Unfortunately, again the lease did not specifically guarantee the continued presence of a runway or Scottish Aviation's continued use of it, even though it might seem like common sense. However, both sleuths noted that in the legal wording there was a specific obligation on the landlord to provide access to the runway. In Scots law, the main rights and obligations contained in a lease can transmit to successors. In the case of the BAe lease, the right and obligations of the landlord were transmitted from the British Government through various Acts of Parliament to the British Airports Authority, a public body, then to BAA plc. The rights and obligations of the tenant were transmitted from Scottish Aviation Limited through its nationalisation by HMG and thence to British Aerospace then to BAe plc. None of this would have prevented BAA from selling to anyone it liked and the buyer would simply inherit BAA's responsibilities as landlord.

However, explained Walton, as a practical matter, having right of access to a runway for 99 years granted by the British Government is a very different thing from a right inherited through purchase by a company. The instant the property was sold, the right of access would be fundamentally weakened because companies can go into liquidation, go out of existence, whereas the British Government is permanent and indestructible and would always be there to enforce the agreed right. In essence, BAe's position would be considerably weakened by a sale to a private company.

"We developed the argument along the lines that the reason Scottish Aviation was willing to go along with the compulsory purchase and enter into the lease containing the right of access in 1953 was because of the permanent and indestructible character of the landlord — the British Government," continued Walton. "Such special character is called in Scots law Delectus Persona and contracts containing clauses with such a character cannot be assigned to a third party. You can compare it to you having a contract with Rembrandt to paint your portrait for a large fee — you wouldn't want him to pass the job on to someone else less skilled."

The question was: would this argument be strong enough to persuade BAA to deal with BAe and their partner ACAP? "Probably not, unless we had some real authority behind it," said Walton. So he suggested, and Allan Macdonald authorised, a consultation with a leading advocate. They decided to test the argument by seeking an opinion from independent senior counsel Brian Gill QC, now Lord Gill, Lord Justice Clerk.

Walton recalled: "It was our intention to wave a senior counsel's opinion in front of BAA and make them realise that we could prevent their sale to their chosen buyer through an interim interdict while we all became embroiled in an interminable, technical and very expensive legal dispute through the courts."

In the event, after several hours of consultation and spirited debate in his chambers with Walton and Hudson, an initially sceptical Brian Gill finally agreed that their argument, whilst somewhat problematic, was "at least stateable", and he wrote a formal opinion to that effect. This was what they needed. A stateable case that BAA, as the successor to the legal obligations of HMG under the statute privatising the British Airports Authority, was obliged to keep the runway open for access. BAe now had clout and were no longer simple tenants at the mercy of their landlord.

"We had them," said Hudson.

5 PIK

Chapter 6
Bargaining
Begins

THEY had the legal argument. That was the easy part. Now ACAP and BAe Prestwick had to convince the BAA and BAe top brass in London that it could affect their decision for the future of Prestwick. BAA now appeared to have two options: sell the airport or close the airport and develop the land. If they chose the latter they could face an embarrassing legal and political battle which could only turn out badly for them and the government. They were going to have to sell.

However, by late summer it looked as if BAA had decided that if they had to sell it would not be to Hudson's group, even though they were backed by George Younger. They would sell to someone hand-picked who would develop the airport's lands and who would not try to bring about the renaissance that Hudson proposed. Peter Kaye and Gordon Watson, of course, fitted that bill.

During a meeting in August with Sir John Egan, the BAA chief executive, JP Sugden, negotiating for BAA, said he considered the BAe legal rights discovered by Hudson and Walton to be "spurious" and made it clear negotiations were going ahead with Kaye and Watson. It also became clear at this meeting that the Kaye and Watson partnership had been offered "financial incentives" to keep the airport operating in the event of the sale to them going ahead. Younger expressed his concern at this apparent favouritism and asked that ACAP be given the same rights. He also warned Egan and Sugden that BAA would be guilty of a serious lack of judgement if they thought BAe was not prepared to act on its legal claim. At the conclusion of one of his now seemingly-endless meetings with Sugden and Sir John, Hudson, beginning to lose patience, decided to spell out what could happen if they did not take the legal threat seriously. Confrontation between BAA and BAe on this issue would not be good for the airport, he said

Hudson warned that if the sale went ahead to Kaye and Watson, ACAP and BAe would exercise a five-day motion which, based on the Gill opinion letter, would result in them being granted an interim interdict which would lead to prolonged litigation, probably lasting three years, taking appeals into account, during which time the airport might or might not be allowed to be reduced in status to that of a "local airport" which could involve shortening the length of the main runway, to the detriment of freight companies who needed the full 10,200 feet for their operations. By the end of the three years, continued Hudson, if BAA won the litigation it would need to absorb the legal expenses and three years' operating losses, estimated at between £4 million and £8 million and they would then need to market an airport which would have lost a great deal of its value. If it lost, BAA would be required to restore the entire and unfettered use of the second runway including re-installation of the lights for night-time operations and continue to operate the whole until 2052.

He went on to make a "one-time" offer to buy the shares of Prestwick Airport Ltd, the BAA subsidiary, for £2.75million, while offering, in return, release of all the BAe historic documents which would allow BAA to make a claim against the government for the difference between the ACAP offer and what they would have received from other bidders.

In a curt response, Sugden ignored the offer, saying he was not prepared to discuss the legal situation with BAe, nor was he prepared to speculate on future developments with Kaye and Watson. However, he asked for clarification of the joint bid with BAe, of which he claimed to have no knowledge and for clarification of ACAP's financial position, the source and certainty of their cash, which showed for the first time he was starting to treat ACAP as a serious player.

The yo-yoing continued into September when, at yet another meeting with Sir Dick Evans and Sir John Egan, Matthew got the strong impression BAA still wanted to close the airport, to knock out any competition with Glasgow and Edinburgh. A "health warning" from Sir Norman Payne, the chair of BAA plc, to potential buyers that the airport was not viable and would be very difficult to run, angered the ACAP team as they felt it poisoned the waters they would need to cross when they took over the airport. It had also come to their attention in August that BAA were continuing to sell off land around the airport; more asset-stripping, as they saw it and a further drain on its value. A chunk of airport land on the edge of Monkton was being earmarked for a golfing range and was being sold for a knockdown price of £75,000. In later years, Hudson would try many ways, unsuccessfully, to re-acquire this key site, offering to build the owner a newer, larger facility with more parking elsewhere. Meanwhile, the people around the BAe chief executive did not seem to appreciate just how valuable the legal argument was to their position.

ACAP faced another blow when in September Bob McKinlay, a Scot who was the London-based managing director of the Commercial Aircraft Division of BAe, was put in charge of negotiations for the Prestwick site. He replaced Allan MacDonald, who was said to be too busy with other matters. The Jetstream 41 was going into first production and MacDonald was also heavily involved with the commercial difficulties of the Jetstream 31, which was entering a challenging period because of hard times being faced by commuter operators in the US. ACAP had lost the vital input of the local man, and now BAe appeared to change tack. For the first time it looked as if they might want to "go it alone" in purchasing the whole site, ignoring the previous admittedly-informal agreement between Hudson and MacDonald. There was speculation that BAe had put aside £6million for the deal but this was quickly denied by the company. The plan now appeared to be that BAe could buy the whole site then lease back the airport to ACAP. That was not what the Younger/Hudson team wanted.

Talks, meantime, were continuing between BAA and the Kaye-Watson partnership. However, by the end of September, following pressure from Younger on Dick Evans, Bob McKinlay was looking more favourably on the joint deal with ACAP and he at last told BAA that they would be working exclusively with ACAP in the purchase of the whole site — unless, he said, ACAP could not put together a business plan. If that happened, BAe would "talk to almost anyone".

In early October, the situation had not progressed much further and an extremely frustrated George Younger and Matthew Hudson met with Vernon Murphy and Richard Everitt, BAA solicitor and board member, who told the ACAP chairman and deputy that Kaye and Watson were still favourites with BAA. It was BAA's view, they said, that the duo had more credibility in terms of operating an airport, given Watson's experience as general manager of Scottish Airports for BAA in the mid-1980s. Younger and Hudson pointed out the local consortium had appointed George Giles, general manager at Prestwick until 1988, as their airport operating consultant and that they would be appointing an airport manager not lacking in experience. Giles had many years of senior operational experience at Prestwick and elsewhere, said Younger, in contrast to Watson who, although he had been involved for a period in administration with Scottish Airports, had never managed an airport.

Frustrated at the shilly-shallying, fed up at not being taken seriously by BAA and in view of the continued support for the Kaye-Watson deal, ACAP decided the time had come to play the legal card. Hudson and Walton, acting for BAe and ACAP, prepared the legal papers and lodged an interim interdict application at the Court of Session in Edinburgh. Once that had been done and a first hearing date set down for a few days later, BAA realised, perhaps for the first time, that ACAP and BAe were very serious and that their stateable case could cause BAA and the government not only great embarrassment but a lot of money, when all they now wanted was to get rid of Prestwick Airport. It was enough, finally, to drag BAA to the negotiating table with BAe and ACAP on an exclusive basis, meaning a parting of the ways with their extremely-disappointed prospective buyers, Kaye and Watson. The case was dropped before it came to a court hearing.

By the end of the month, negotiations between BAA and BAe/ACAP were seriously underway and Bob McKinlay was joined by Kim Cohen, head of business development at the Commercial Aircraft Divisions at BAe. However in their talks with BAA at this stage BAe were still holding to the position first mooted by McKinlay that they would buy the whole site and lease back the airport to ACAP on a long-term agreement, probably 99 years. Younger and Hudson still favoured ACAP buying the entire site, selling the factory and the main runway to BAe for a fraction of the market value, and BAe then leasing the runway back to ACAP. It was stalemate.

Meetings continued throughout October, with Cohen calling for details of the ACAP financial situation and demanding to see the major points of Hudson's business plan for operating the airport. By November, BAe were con-

US bank sues for $20m

Airport bid partner in debt case

By DEREK DOUGLAS,
Chief Reporter

A CANADIAN business-
man who is involved with
Royal Bank of Scotland
chairman George Younger,
MP, in an attempt to buy
Prestwick Airport, is being
sued by an American bank
for $20m, encompassing
alleged non-payment of a
construction loan and
recovery of legal fees.

The revelations come as the
airport deal is, apparently, on
the verge of conclusion and amid
claims they are part of a "dirty-
tricks" campaign designed to
blight the chances of the Younger consortium, which is seen in
some quarters as being the current front-runner.

Another consortium involved,
AAP, which includes the former
Scottish Airports managing director, Mr Gordon Watson,
rejects suggestions that it is involved in a smear campaign.
Mr Watson said: "We are not
involved in any kind of 'dirty-
tricks' campaign. We are
involved in getting the future of
Prestwick Airport resolved as
soon as possible."

George Younger

difficulties. He is contesting the
action being brought by the First
Fidelity Bank of New Jersey and
maintains he has been the "fall-
guy" for a deal which went sour.

The bank has now instructed
lawyers in this country and, de-
pending on the outcome of the
American litigation, the case is
set to continue at the Court of
Session in Edinburgh.

Mr Hudson is a director of the
Ayrshire Community Airport
Project Ltd, a company formed
earlier this year to bid for Prestwick Airport, which is to be sold
off by the British Airports'
Authority.

In addition to the local MP,
Mr Younger, the other directors

rison, Mr Robert Macdonald
and Mr Peter Paterson.

Mr Younger, a former De-
fence Secretary and Secretary of
State for Scotland, who has been
the Ayr MP since 1964 has, also,
not filed his ACAP directorship
with the House of Commons
register of members' commercial
and financial interests, although
he maintains his involvement is
common knowledge and that it
had come about after the annual
return of members' interests had
been completed.

Initially, Mr Younger refused
to comment about the First Fidelity case and Mr Hudson. He
declined to respond on whether,
in his capacity as Royal Bank of
Scotland chairman, it caused
him any embarrassment or
whether he was aware of the
court action when he became involved with ACAP.

He said: "I'm sorry, I am not
characteristically unhelpful but I
think I must make no comment
at all on these matters."

However, a short while later
he contacted the Glasgow Herald to say he had taken the
opportunity to consult his
records and that he had, indeed,
known about the First Fidelity
case when he became involved
with the airport project and Mr

A report in *The Glasgow Herald* was
potentially embarrassing for Matthew
Hudson at a crucial time in negotiations for
Prestwick Airport. Hudson was convinced
the timing of the revelations was not
coincidental.

tinuing to demand more details of Hudson's business model, including the multi-skilled strategy with minimum staffing levels. Hudson felt that Cohen and his associates in business development were more interested in learning his ideas and how they would work than in the future of Prestwick Airport. Angered at this, Hudson contacted Younger who, in his diplomatic way, asked whether BAe were not perhaps "straying beyond the boundaries" of the original agreement. In other words, ACAP's detailed plans for running the airport were not their concern. BAe, as he understood it, should be interested in preserving their existing investment at Prestwick, principally the Jetstream programme, including the flying college, and not in the business of running the airport, which would be ACAP's concern. In a letter to Bob McKinlay, Younger pointed out that the agreement they were drawing up over the runway would save BAe money.

He said: "We have clearly understood our role in providing this protection to extend to the provision of guaranteed flying from Prestwick at an economic price for so long as BAe or any successor requires it." This protection would represent a saving of about £500,000 a year to BAe. His letter continued: "As a matter of commercial prudence, however, we are not prepared to provide BAe with additional financial information regarding ACAP, its funding or its business plans unless these matters directly impact the preservation of your own investment at Prestwick. Information relating to our own risks and returns are matters for our board of directors and our investors."

He asked for Heads of Agreement to be completed without delay as time was running short. Working in consultation with Hudson he went on to offer BAe £2 million for the airport upon completion of their transaction with BAA. This would be a back-to-back deal with BAe buying the whole site up front and ACAP immediately buying the airport from them. The £2 million would cover the freehold title to all the assets being discussed, with the exception of the BAe site and the runway. ACAP would gain a 99-year lease of the runway, which they would maintain and repair. They would also enter into operating contracts with BAe for flying rights.

Just as it seemed the deal was coming together at last, another cloud appeared on the horizon. A newspaper reporter was tipped off that there might be something worth looking into in Hudson's background. As a result, a story appeared on November 11, 1991, in the Glasgow Herald headed "Airport bid partner in debt case; US bank sues for $20 million." The story claimed the First Fidelity Bank of New Jersey was suing Hudson, alleging non-payment of a construction loan and recovery of legal fees. Hudson immediately suspected there might be dirty tricks going on in a bid to blight the chances of the group who were now seen as front-runners in the airport bid, though AAP immediately issued a statement through Gordon Watson rejecting any suggestion that his group had anything to do with the story. He said: "We are not involved in any kind of dirty tricks campaign. We are involved in getting the future of Prestwick Airport resolved as soon as possible."

The newspaper report said that the case being brought against Hudson involved a principal sum of $11,814,807 which, it was claimed, was the residue of a $15 million loan granted to his Market Towers Associates property company in 1983. The loan was for the construction of a 14-storey condominium project known as the Marina Club of Atlantic City, New Jersey. The First Fidelity Bank alleged that the borrowers defaulted on their obligations, leaving Hudson liable for the unpaid portion of the outstanding loan together with interest, costs, expenses and legal fees. According to their lawyer acting for First Fidelity the total amount being claimed was $20,047,590.

According to the report, the bank pursued the case through the American courts and a written opinion showed the only outstanding point was current ownership of the Marina Club project and whether the value of the property should be deducted from the total sum owed.

The Edinburgh law firm McGrigor Donald was instructed to pursue the case in Edinburgh and in normal Hudson style, he hit back immediately. Being fully aware of the impact such dirty tricks could have on the fragile negotiations, he wrote to the directors of ACAP to give them chapter and verse on the background to the case, in addition to asking his US lawyer to write to the board in order to give them an impartial and accurate history of events. Hudson told his board that in the early 1980s he had worked with Atlantic City in New Jersey to create affordable housing in the black community. Over a period of several years he had assembled an eight-acre site in the marina area of the city. He obtained all local, state and federal approvals for 1200 units. He was then asked by the Atlantic City Housing Authority to construct the first building of some 212 condominium flats. In order to help with the financial risk involved in such a project, he arranged a 50/50 partnership with a UK property plc which was experienced in American business. Construction financing for the building was arranged with a bank and, as is usual in transactions on this scale, business guarantees were sought for the funding. The UK company gave a full faith and credit corporate guarantee. Hudson also gave a personal guarantee although he had been assured — and the documents stated — that its sole purpose was to ensure his personal attention during the construction phase only of the project, a so-called construction guarantee. In any event, at this time the value of the eight acres of land or the building on its own would far outstrip the construction loan. The building was constructed on time and on budget and pre-sold as to more than 60 per cent. However, due to a failure of America's leading title insurance company days before the legal title to the condominium units was to take place, followed subsequently by significant downturn in the housing market in the Atlantic City area, the project was ultimately unsuccessful.

In 1985, when Hudson moved to the UK to pursue another business opportunity, the bank in the US dealing with the Atlantic City property had appeared to be satisfied with the way the matter was being handled. The UK company had been taken over by its lenders and the chairman eventually charged with fraud. A fresh loan agreement was sent out to Hudson to sign and although he did this, unprofessional practices across the water in the US, he said, saw the document being altered; his signature was removed and attached to a new document — one which deleted the UK company as guarantor. In 1986 the bank decided to take legal action against Hudson to get their money back for the construction loan. He obtained legal advice both in the UK and in America and strongly defended his position. The matter was eventually resolved without liability to Hudson. The ACAP board gave him their full backing. Hudson was convinced the timing of the revelations was not coincidental, and he told the Herald: "I am the vulnerable one. They can't get to George Younger but they think they can get at me. I am the stooge. I'm also the spark plug of this operation and if you take away the spark plug then the car doesn't work very well."

As Christmas 1991 approached, outline terms were being agreed for the seamless transition from BAA to BAe to ACAP in the back-to-back deal, despite further intervention from Kaye and Watson, who said they felt "betrayed" by Younger. At this late stage they were still talking of entering into negotiations with ACAP and BAe to acquire and manage Prestwick as a commercial operation and were bitter that their approaches, including an offer of £4.75 million for the airport, had met with a "peremptory negative". A date, however, was set for the agreements to be signed with ACAP and BAe on January 10, with the takeover scheduled for April 1. "It seemed appropriate," observed Hudson. "Everybody said we were fools, so April Fools Day it was."

There was still a great deal of three-way negotiating to do, though, especially for Hudson and his new team of solicitors. BAe and BAA, of course, had the largest Scottish firms on tap. The smallest of the contestants would have to be nimble and work harder to come out ahead. Symbolically perhaps, the last transatlantic flight under BAA management took off from Prestwick on December 9, 1991. It was an Air Transat Lockheed bound for Toronto.

ACAP were on course to buy the airport, now they had to raise the cash to complete the deal. They were going to have to find £2 million to pay BAe, who in turn had agreed to pay BAA a knockdown price of £1.75million for the entire site — so much for the "spurious" legal situation. It has been estimated that Kaye and Watson had been prepared to pay up to £9 million for the site, thanks to its development potential. Now that the dust was beginning to settle, it was clear BAe would make £250,000 from the transaction and gain the freehold of their site, their factory and the main runway. "A pretty good deal that I helped them make," said Hudson. For their £2million ACAP were to receive the terminal, parking area, control tower, second runway, the crash and rescue centre, ancillary freight buildings, a lease of the main runway and such ancillary land as BAA had not sold or otherwise encumbered, such as the Freeport and the driving range.

Hudson had asked the original board members to each pledge £50,000 for their shares in the company. Sir David McNee had been a public servant his whole life; navy in WWII and then the police, so his contribution of £25,000 was provided by Hudson. Younger had also been a public servant much of his life after the army so it was agreed that he would put no money into the company upfront but once he was retired from politics would contribute his director's fees as his capital contribution.

How to raise the rest? Hudson had agreed to underwrite the funding but he was a staunch believer in two good Scots principles: use OPM (other people's money) and "You cannot have too much working capital available."

So his first port of call was to Kyle and Carrick District Council. Councillor Ian Welsh and Eddie Clark had been involved in the tri-party negotiations, reporting regularly back to the council members who were now working on how they could best contribute to the successful future of the airport. In November, ACAP had asked for a holiday for business rates — a massive £250,000 a year — in respect of the airport if they were successful in their bid. The council chief executive, Ian Smillie, said that the holiday was not possible but a council-sanctioned reduction of £100,000 brought the figure down to a more manageable £150,000. The council was also prepared to buy the terminal building from the company and lease it back for a nominal sum. This would be no loss to the ratepayers because of the interesting way local government finance was conducted. Provided the lease would exceed 20 years, the council could generate a capital receipt equivalent from the government to the value of the building. This resulted in a £1 million loan to ACAP from Kyle and Carrick District

Council. The council also took 100,000 ordinary £1 shares in the company, plus a seat on the board and a Golden Share which would allow the council some input in decisions affecting the future development of the airport.

Hudson next turned to the larger authority, Strathclyde Regional Council, which was also keen to support the airport buyout. Now that Glasgow was settled into its role of BAA's centre of operations in Scotland, the huge regional authority, which was based in the city, realised, if belatedly, they had some responsibility towards the Ayrshire airport and its workers. After some negotiation, with the help of Sir David McNee who was first Chief Constable of Strathclyde and who had retained good relations with the senior Labour councillors, and with the backing of Prestwick Regional Councillor John Baillie, the region agreed to lend £1.5 million, with the cargo house and freight sheds as security.

Councillor Ian Welsh said: "What that in fact meant was that the public sector funded the purchase price of the airport, the actual money paid to BAA and BAe. It was done without risk because the airport now had a future based on the Hudson operating model. The vehicle was ACAP but the council ended up as guardians. Our role was that of facilitators. We had a clear vision of what we wanted for the airport and we did two things: we structured the sale and lease-back deal which meant we could capitalise £5 million of cash and we also helped organise the loan from Strathclyde Regional Council. The myth locally was that the band of local businessmen saved the airport — but they couldn't have done it without the council. In turn, I have to admit Matthew did the job the council couldn't do. He saved the airport and secured the jobs of the workers out there."

ACAP also borrowed back £250,000 from BAe, their profit from the buyout deal, while Blanefield Investments, Hudson's family company, also put in another £175,000 to go with the costs it had incurred between the beginning of his involvement in 1990 and April 1992. They had the money, now the deal had to be finalised.

On February 13, 1992, ACAP went public, announcing the three-sided deal with BAA and BAe, though, behind the scenes, negotiations were far from complete. Dotting the Is and crossing the Ts was to take a further six or so weeks, with the three sets of lawyers and their clients working around the clock as the official take-over date of April 1 approached. The smallest team of lawyers, Kenneth Christie and Morag Campbell of the Glasgow legal firm McClure Naismyth, had but one client — Matthew Hudson, who was driving from his home near Kirkoswald in Ayrshire to Glasgow at 6am every day and back again at midnight or later.

However on that February day, a delighted George Younger, in his role as chairman of the consortium, told the country's assembled media that this was a milestone for Prestwick and for Scotland and announced that the new company would be called PIK Limited, after the internationally-recognised call sign for Prestwick Airport, used by aviators and the aviation industry. The airport would be known as Prestwick International, he said, and under the new owners it would work to regain its position as a major transatlantic and pan-European hub. They had been working close on two years, he said, to secure a safe future for the airport, during which time they had commissioned a number of feasibility studies which gave them confidence that the airport's fortunes could be turned around. Initial efforts would be made to attract more freight business as well as rebuilding the chartered passenger business which had been a significant feature of the airport in the past. "We cannot guarantee instant success but as a non-conurbation airport with two runways and an excellent environment we have tremendous potential," he said.

Younger , a proud chairman of the new company, had seen his dream realised and Hudson was his deputy. During that time as they entered into serious negotiating mode, Hudson was regularly flying to London, staying four nights a week, and the experience made him determined to ensure that Prestwick would improve the services available to Scots seeking to travel to the capital. "I got very aggravated at the high fares British Airways were charging, I can tell you. It cost £212 to go on the Shuttle. I said to myself, if this airport deal gets done, at the very least Scots and tourists are going to get cheap flights to and from London."

Although busy with the lawyers five days a week, Hudson and his ACAP partners also had to turn their attention to employing staff to run the airport. And they didn't have much time to get the right team together. It was mid-February, and six weeks before they were due to open for business. Hudson had already written detailed job descriptions for every position required by his new business model. As part of the negotiated agreement, he had required that the remaining airport staff were to be made redundant by BAA, which would fully protect their redundancy payments and pension rights. ACAP then planned to re-hire, as fresh, the people they wanted to keep on. It was a clean sheet, said Hudson. Not one of the previous jobs existed. His vision had wiped the slate clean. Not one job would be the same after midnight March 31, 1992. There had been 71 full-time and 20 part-time airport staff that January. The plan now was to open for business with a full-time team of 51.

Mike Dooley, a previous manager at Prestwick under BAA, had been persuaded to return from Gibraltar, where he was airport manager, to run the new airport set-up. Hudson brought in Vince Coogins, who operated an employment agency in Ayr so that ACAP could take advantage of training grants. By running training programmes for new staff, the first three months' salary would be paid by the government. Hudson said: "If Vince Coogins hadn't existed I would have to have invented him. I said to Vince, 'I'm not going to hire anybody, you're going to hire them, put them in training, first in classrooms and then at the airport and the government's going to pay for it.'"

It was important at this stage they saved every penny they could. They had no aviation revenue, there were no passenger flights and the only freight business came from the once-a-night Fedex DC8s that touched down for refuelling.

Meanwhile, Coopers & Lybrand Deloitte were performing due diligence work at the airport on behalf of BAe, going over all the details of the acquisition with a fine toothcomb. Even at this late stage BAA was proving difficult, refusing access to the computer systems, denying Hudson access to inspect non-public areas of the airport facilities and refusing his request to speak to the staff. Neither Coopers & Lybrand Deloitte nor anyone connected with ACAP were to be allowed to conduct interviews with the computer staff until the final details of the deal were concluded, just before the takeover.

CLD, however, had another concern. They were worried, as were the CAA at this stage, that Hudson's working plan of employing a tight team of multi-skilled personnel would not be effective in running the airport efficiently and, perhaps more importantly, could they do it safely? It had never been done before. Most concern centred on the Crash Rescue Service. The business plan was revolutionary and untested. Hudson said: "We were going to have a one-core team throughout the airport. We were going to do everything; one level of overheads, one accounting system, one set of insurance, one, one, one. We were going to be a team, but a proud team.

"Normally an airline might negotiate between 20 and 40 contracts and deal with that many vendors to operate from an airport. At Prestwick you were only going to have to deal with one, and that was myself. That way I felt the customer would get a better service. The prevailing wisdom when I explained this to anybody who had any knowledge of airports was, 'Ye cannae dae that!' I had to show them that I could."

He had to learn how a big international airport operated and that was where the experience of George Giles, a former BAA manager at Prestwick, would be invaluable. Giles was the ultimate consultant, incredibly knowledgeable, open and helpful, Hudson found.

One of the main drivers in the revolutionary multi-skilling plan was integrating the Crash Rescue Service personnel which, at that time, was an independent culture at the airport. Hudson said: "They talked to no one else, they had their own separate entrance, their own private facilities more than a mile from the terminal with leather armchairs, televisions, movies and a billiards table. The service was very expensive to operate and its revenue output was zero. They were strictly a cost centre and my model didn't allow for cost centres, my business model only allowed for profit centres." Hudson's plan for every member of staff employed by ACAP to have two skills — a revenue skill and a safety skill — applied also to the crash/rescue team. Safety was essential, but so was profitablility. Tackling the Crash Rescue Service was not going to be straight-forward, Hudson recognised. "Not only did they produce no revenue, they produced no sense of camaraderie, no sense of team. I had all these able-bodied men who weren't part of what I and the others were going to be doing."

When Hudson presented his idea for a multi-skilled force to the CAA they were predictably discouraging and warned him to anticipate opposition from the unions. Hudson, however, was of the view that the unions were more interested in keeping the airport open than in their presumed rights "to sit in leather chairs and do nothing". The CAA remained unconvinced. Hudson made a tactical retreat to consolidate his proposals, convinced he could persuade the CAA his plan was workable.

The core of the problem was that the fire-rescue people had to be able to get from where they were at any time to the furthest part of the airport fence in two minutes flat, fully kitted-up and with a stated amount of equipment — foam essentially. They couldn't just skoot across in a little pick-up, because the equipment regulations ruled that out. So Hudson pored over large maps of the airport (BAA wouldn't give him detailed plans of the area) and hammered out some convincing calculations before returning to the CAA to demonstrate how it could be done. "I showed the CAA my calculations. I showed them that my proposals actually made for a safer airport. Much safer. After a while they realised that: (a) I was right; and (b) I wasn't going away. Then they became cautious supporters. That was gratifying. I always found the safety branch of the CAA to be safety-minded, pragmatic and candid."

The plan was simple. Crash Rescue Service would be relocated from where they had been living in cosy isolation to a new building adjacent to the main apron. From their new base, they could still make the perimeter within the required two minutes. They would be employed on the apron, loading and unloading freight and eventually baggage, but it was agreed that when work-ing on the freighters — they had no passenger flights at this time — none of the core crew that needed to be on the "two minutes to the furthest perimeter" response team would go inside the planes. Eventually, the CAA agreed it could work. Hudson had them on-side. He felt they were secretly pleased to have one over on the unions. Next, he had to work on the members of the Crash Rescue crew who were returning to work at the airport after the takeover and who understandably were not happy with the new structure. They had been an elite, well-paid group and they were not going to give up that status easily. Now, instead of being exclusively firemen, training part of the time and watching movies or playing pool or sleeping the rest of the time, they would be expected to be ramp handlers and operate the ramp equipment — their revenue skill.

Shortly after April 1, a stormy meeting was held and the Crash Rescue crew, led by two of the prior BAA firemen, decided to rebel against Hudson's oper-ating model as it applied to them. "They gave an ultimatum to Mike Dooley, the new managing director, who was a former BAA man, and he wouldn't go down to the ramp and cross it to their building to confront them," said Hudson. "I was there in a small office down the hall, keeping a watchful eye on what was going on, so I did his job. Out I went to listen to their complaints. Then I explained to them that their threat to walk off the job was just fine with me. I would write to the other employees of the airport telling them to explain to their families how they would no longer have a job and the airport would be closed because the Crash Rescue team would not agree to the new operating model that they and the others had signed up for. I pointed out that I would send the same letter to their wives. My wife, I noted, would be ecstatic, as she hadn't seen much of me for the best part of two years at that point. I gave them 15 minutes to decide and if I didn't have a small delegation in the MD's office in that time to signify they were on the team, I would be getting the letters out that night as my secretary was standing by.

"The delegation arrived within the required 15 minutes. The mini-crisis was resolved. Two of the fire-rescue crew left shortly after that. Meanwhile, other staff were signed up and were sent on courses to get CAA-approved Crash Rescue and fire-fighting service qualifications. Soon we had a marvellous bunch of stalwarts who became some of my staunchest supporters."

The team was coming together. By November the Crash Rescue team had their own new state-of-the-art premises when a new £200,000 apron vehicle maintenance and storage facility was opened, the first major development at the airport since 1964. It included a new fire station which held the two new six-wheel Javelin appliances.

It wasn't just the fire-rescue team that found themselves doing more than one job. The multi-skilling applied right across the board. As the airport business developed and passengers started arriving, secretaries would double as check-in staff; they would also serve at the duty-free, then return to their desks to continue with their "real" jobs.

PIK

Chapter 7
How To Run
An Airport

SOME people shook hands, some didn't. It was 5am April Fools Day 1992 and the deal finally was done. The buyout was complete. ACAP owned the airport while BAe had their factory site and ownership of the runway, which they were leasing back to the airport. PIK Ltd was in business, just over two years after it looked as if the airport was destined to close following the Open Skies decision.

Richard Everitt, the senior BAA representative sent north to handle the deal was, said Matthew Hudson, a true gentleman, and the day before the transaction he joked that he hoped he was not going to have to take Prestwick back from ACAP the following week.

"I said: 'Why don't you sell Edinburgh to me while you are at it because you know you don't like Edinburgh. It's never going to make you too much money. I'll be happy to do that deal next week.' He just laughed," said Hudson. That would have been perfect. If I had had Prestwick and Edinburgh we would have been set. We could have played a very nice tune with those two instruments."

There were kisses and hugs all round, even though the exhausted ACAP team had been working into the small hours. In fact, the ACAP lawyer Morag Campbell had been up for 48 hours straight because there had been a title problem and she had had to bring in a former senior conveyancing colleague to tie up the details at the last minute.

Hudson said: "BAA just wouldn't let me look at things in the airport and they wouldn't let me look at any of the leases until we were well into the negotiations. However it all worked out. Two days before conclusion these leases finally turned up in cardboard boxes. I went straight up to the conference room at the lawyers' offices and within half an hour I had struck paydirt. I found the leases with the fuel companies. I had had my suspicions about what had been happening there over the years. HMG as landlord on the one side, up against the major oil companies on the other and it must have seemed a backwater to both sides. No one who cared about the airport had read these leases in decades. When I read them, I knew we had struck gold. By the time I was finished negotiating with the oil companies, two years later, we had more cash and operating value from them than we had paid for the airport."

But that was for later. On the morning of April 1 the ACAP team again welcomed the nation's press who for once were going to have to print a good-news story about Prestwick Airport. The consortium members did interviews, posed for photographs, appeared on television and relished the moment, for they knew the hard work was just beginning. Hudson had a particular reason for wanting to get home on that day. While he had been tied up in negotiations, his wife Pamela

Previous page: Celebrating the successful Prestwick Airport buyout deal is Bill Miller, George Younger and George Giles *Photograph courtesy of Mirrorpix*

had also been busy, giving birth to the couple's second child, Matthew, who arrived on March 28. "So we had a real celebration on April 1. Pammy and the baby came with the winning team to a restaurant in nearby Girvan. I can even remember the wine we had — inexpensive but very tasty. A bit like Prestwick. I had two new babies to celebrate," said Hudson, a proud new dad and airport owner. They savoured the moment. Now the talking was over and they were running an airport. The new team took over the airport at 1am and Hudson was there to see the hand-over. By 8am the new sign "Prestwick International — Scotland's Airport" was already going up, with unions convener Willie Poole supervising.

BAA had kept Hudson off the airport premises during the final stages of the negotiations, although he had managed to sneak in to the freight-loading area one late night, with the help of some airport staff in the February, just after the announcement of the buyout. Now that the airport was his, he toured every part, scoured every nook and cranny with a tape recorder in hand. "I don't think anyone had ever done that before," he said. "I knew every part of every building when I had finished."

Hudson knew he needed to have the workforce on side and that meant facing up to the unions. Just before he took over the airport there had been six unions, and only 71 workers. That situation couldn't be sustained. With everyone made redundant by BAA, all of Hudson's crew were new hires, and there were no unions. He had earlier identified the unions' convener Willie Poole, who had spent his adult life at the airport, and gained his confidence. "Willie was Mr Union so I sought him out early on," said Hudson. "I liked him immediately and I said to him: 'What's more important to you, saving the unions or saving the airport?' He quickly realised — no airport, no jobs, no unions."

Hudson offered Poole a key role in the new management team. It was new times, new ideas. Poole had been involved in the struggle to save the airport and remembered the shock of the first redundancies after Open Skies. "We were sitting at a consultative committee meeting and the general manager said there would be 100 pay-offs. We knew then the writing was on the wall. One runway was shut then the next manager Lesley Bale tried to sell the second runway to the farmer who had been renting it. We were really worried. Then I was approached by Matthew Hudson who gave me the outline of his plans to save the airport and asked for my support. BAA had wanted me to transfer to Glasgow, but I decided to stay at Prestwick because I believed in what Matthew was trying to do," said Poole.

"It was a really difficult situation. Matthew said he wanted to work with a team of 51. We had firemen who were firemen and nothing else. They didn't come out of their shed unless there was a fire. We had to talk to engineers, electricians and explain that everyone had to be multi-skilled. Where in the past we had set hours of working now we would have to work hours to suit the airport. But the workers did it, because they wanted to save their airport as well as their jobs. We had to become caterers, we had to run bars, work in the duty-free, do the cleaning. And we did it."

Hudson agreed there could be unions at the airport, but not six — two. It was eventually agreed they would have the IPMS (the air traffic controllers' union) and the T&G. He also warned he was not the type of boss who indulged in long talks and negotiations over cups of tea. "I said to Willie: 'We are going to have to work this out. Talk to your men and once we are in a position to talk seriously let's invite the heads of the unions to come and meet us.'"

By this time Poole had been appointed engineering manager in charge of training and Hudson reminded him that he was now a manager and he would have to think about his position during the talks — the workers had been used to him being a union man.

They had their meeting in the conference room at the airport on April 3, two days after the takeover. It was attended by the six union shop stewards, their six deputies, STUC general secretary Campbell Christie and his deputy. All 14 were on one side of the table facing Poole and Hudson on the other. Hudson told Christie that he supported the concept of unions if they did a good job for the workforce, but his job was to save the airport. "I said a union was supportable or perhaps two, so as to include the air traffic control staff, as I had it in my master plan to take that over, too — once I convinced NATS [National Air Travel Services] to go. I said I would help them organise, but I didn't want confrontation. If they wanted the jobs they needed to work together with me and my management team for the good of the airport." Eventually, Christie and his executives agreed to the two unions; they all wanted to keep the airport open. In general, the union compromise worked well, said Hudson. "People were our strength and that includes Campbell Christie and his colleagues."

Some workers who didn't like the new set-up left and others regarded Poole as a traitor for joining the management team. But most stayed. Despite Hudson's management style, there was no doubt that he was fully engaged. "BAA were losing money and they were overstaffed," he said. "As a result the workers didn't have much to do. I had a lot I wanted them to do and I didn't want to pay them as much since we simply couldn't afford to in the early days. With BAA, nobody checked if you were doing your job. I checked. Some didn't want to work like that and they left. Willie then asked how would they be replaced and I said they wouldn't. Word soon got round and things settled down. My attitude was if you don't want to work here, please don't. Better you should decide that than me. I believe in management by walking around. I spent a lot of time walking around seeing how things were being done, praising as often as I could and making helpful suggestions when I couldn't.

"This was new for everybody, but the unions were nothing but positive. They could have caused me trouble. I didn't want to fight with the unions because they represented a large segment of the Scottish population. The disappointing thing

Prestwick's large runway is able to accommodate the world's largest airplane, the Antonov AN-225 Mriya, pictured here during take-off in June 2007 *Photo courtesy of dtimages@hotmail.co.uk*

was that once we got out in the field and kicking the ball, it wasn't the unions that caused us problems — it was government. Not local government but higher up. When we started we were dealing with Strathclyde Region and some of them were not as helpful as they could have been; they had been wined and dined by BAA for too long, I think. The Scottish Office, not withstanding that George Younger had been there, were a dead loss. Ian Lang, the new Scottish Secretary, did nothing for us. When we opened the rail station which we paid for and designed and built, George said we should invite him so I did, but it was through gritted teeth. I told George: 'The next time he does something for us will be the first time.' They were solidly in the BAA camp, all those old school tie types. "

Having reached a deal with the unions, Hudson now turned his attention to Strathclyde Police. There was a dedicated police station at the airport and it was not cheap to operate. According to Hudson, BA had been paying them hundreds of thousands of pounds a year without really checking on what they were getting for their money. This was very much not the new boss's style of doing business. "Strathclyde Police charged a fortune and I still don't know what it was based on. All I know is that we got a couple of constables who, it seemed to me, used to stand around smoking cigarettes. It was a lot of money and I told them we were not paying. They insisted we had to pay and the bills kept mounting. I just didn't pay them. In fact, I told them they were lucky I didn't charge them for having these two chaps loitering about the airport."

At this point, with PIK facing the prospect of being sued by the police, the former boss of the Met and PIK director Sir David McNee stepped in. He took Matthew to a meeting at police HQ in Glasgow with Strathclyde Chief Constable, Leslie Sharpe. Hudson explained the new set-up at the airport and the fact they had no passengers. This meant they did not require a 24/7 police presence on the premises. Plus, he added, the Prestwick town police station was only a few minutes away.

Thanks to Sir David's intervention, an agreement was reached that the six officers assigned to the airport would be withdrawn, along with their large salaries and cover would be provided by the town section – however, a small office for use as a police post in emergencies would be maintained. Police would also continue to be represented on the Airport Security Committee. It was agreed that the airport would be policed as part of a normal patrol and would be given the same police response as any other business in the area. However, if the officers were required to deal with aircraft emergencies or ground incidents, PIK would meet the cost. These changes would be reviewed every year and peace would reign for a further four years.

Numerous cost-cutting measures were introduced in the early days. Willie Poole remembers the grass round the runways had to be kept to a certain height because of wildlife. A local gardening firm had been attending to that, but the job of grass-cutting was added to the crash-rescue team's list of duties. "They didn't like it, but we had to cut costs," said Poole. Then he had a brainwave. He contacted a local farmer who paid *them* to graze his stock on the land – problem solved.

Scottish Power carried out the maintenance of the runways lighting, but Poole re-trained some of his own men to the same standard and saved the airport £20,000 a year. "We did lots of things like that. Money was ploughed back into the airport instead of into someone else's pocket," said Poole.

Now it was time for Hudson to take charge of the other services and start making money. They had to raise any money they could, and as a result were taking all sorts of unusual bookings. This was the early 1990s, and all-night raves were popular. The large empty terminal building was an ideal venue and it quickly became extremely popular for these teenage events.

One of the first areas to be targeted in the new business plan was catering. The contract which had been in place before ACAP took over was not renewed, but the woman who had been running the catering became PIK's new catering manager; a quick fix, but the airport's first big public relations disaster lay ahead.

Ayrshire Chamber of Commerce and Industry had booked the terminal building for their annual dinner, mainly since it was the only building in the area that could comfortably take the thousand or so guests they were expecting. The new catering manager was confident the booking could be handled. The equip-

The running of the duty-free shop was a classic example of running operations the Matthew Hudson way
Photograph courtesy of Phil Toman

ment was there and as long as they could rent enough heated trolleys to store the cooked meals, there should be no reason for concern. The fact that the food had to be prepared on the first floor while the tables were set out in the main concourse was not an insurmountable problem. The food would be prepared and taken down to the concourse in the rented heated cars where it would keep warm until served. Unfortunately, although the heated trolleys were working when they were checked at 5pm, 30 minutes later, five of the six trolleys were cold. Panic stations. The guests were due to arrive in a couple of hours, and since it was not possible to find replacement trolleys, the only remaining option was to bring down whatever cookers were available from the restaurant so that the food could be put on them in an effort to keep it warm.

"It didn't work," said Hudson. "It took about an hour and a half to serve everybody their main course. When they got the food it was cold. It was a complete disaster." Worse, every important person in the Ayrshire business community was there. "We had to give them their money back and there was a terrible credibility problem. It was the worst thing I can remember happening during my time at the airport, and I vowed it would never happen again." A letter went out to everyone who attended the dinner giving an explanation of what had happened and a promise that there would be a full enquiry — which there was. But the damage was done.

So it was time to re-assess the catering. Hudson brought in his home catering expert: his wife Pamela, whose remit was to run the bars and restaurants and make them a popular attraction. Although they still had only freighters coming in, Hudson wanted to return to the good old days when the airport was centre of the Ayrshire social scene. He wanted people to come back out to Prestwick for food and drink. "We didn't have much in the way of planes to offer them but we could offer a good place for a night out."

Two empty shops on the main concourse were to be converted into a bar. With budget restraints still very much in force, there were limited funds for the alterations, so the natural rough-sawn pine wall panelling was stripped from behind the upper mezzanine signs and used to line the walls of the check-in desks. The new theme bar would cash in on Prestwick's Elvis connection, recalling the occasion when the King had touched down at the neighbouring USAF base. On one of their trips to the USA, the Hudsons had picked up some Elvis memorabilia, and so the Graceland Bar was born.

So there were no passengers yet... but that did not mean that a duty-free shop was a bad idea. Prestwick had, after all, been the first Scottish airport to be given the go-ahead to sell duty-free whisky in 1959. Hudson approached fellow board member and wine merchant Tim Morrison, asking him to make a report of duty-free facilities for the ACAP board. Surprisingly, it made dismal reading. During 1990 and 1991, Morrison told the board, the duty-free industry had suffered one of the biggest sales downturns in its history. There had been a big drop in the number of visitors from the USA, blamed largely on the Gulf War, but tourism had also witnessed a large drop in the number of Japanese visitors to the UK. Duty-free retailers would be looking to trim costs, he warned. However, the PIK board agreed that any airport looking to attract passengers could not run without a duty-free Shop.

Before BAA's scaled rundown of services at Prestwick, the duty-free turnover at the airport in 1989 had amounted to £2.7 million. This was with a throughput of approximately 300,000 passengers. It was clearly a market worth pursuing. Hudson returned to his model of providing all airport services in-house and set about making arrangements for his staff to provide duty free facilities, despite the by now familiar opposition from traditionalists. Running duty-free was too complicated, particularly without an experienced staff, the experts alleged.

At that time, Air Rianta were regarded as world leaders in this field, the highly-successful operation at Dublin being held up regularly as an example of industry best. Hudson studied how they operated, then consulted various friends and, in particular, Tim Morrison, who advised him on the best drinks to stock up on. He advised Hudson to concentrate on specialty whiskies, especially malts. The disadvantage to this approach, though, he warned, might be that it would tie up considerable sums of cash in stock, and moving it might be unpredictable, considering the lack of passengers. A suggestion that traders and agents might leave stock on a consignment basis, which would be paid for on sale, did not meet with much enthusiasm from either traders or agents. There was a similar reaction from the big distilling companies. However, Morrison was sure they would make a profit in the long run if they were prepared to invest the cash.

Hudson then turned to his other expert, his wife Pamela, for advice about beauty products for women, particularly perfumes, the second-most popular product for duty-free shoppers. With cigarettes and cigars, plus a wide selection of Scottish souvenirs and knitwear added to the stock list, the shop was almost ready to open. Using his in-house staffing strategy, Hudson re-assigned Alison Black, one of his three secretaries, to the task of running the new facility. In November 1992, seven months after the airport takeover, the departing Italy football team and their entourage were the first guests in Prestwick International's duty-free shop. The Italians had flown into Prestwick in a chartered aircraft for their World Cup qualifier against Scotland at Ibrox on November 18 and in the space of one hour £2,500 worth of goods had been sold, including alcohol, perfumes and Scottish lambswool sweaters. It was a promising start.

Allison Black ran the duty-free successfully with great help from other crew members. When the shop became busy, the secretaries and other members of staff would move in to help out as the passengers moved through, then they returned to get on with their normal work. The range of goods on sale increased over the years as the passengers increased, and by the time the airport was sold in 1998 the duty-free sales per passenger were in excess of Air Rienta. It was also reported that they offered the lowest prices in the UK.

PIK

Chapter 8
Trouble In
The Tower

IN JANUARY 1992, just before the takeover, National Air Traffic Services (a part of the CAA) dropped a bombshell. They announced they would be withdrawing their services for local air traffic facilities at Prestwick from midnight on March 31 the following year unless the airport agreed to make payments to them. Another April Fools' event, said Matthew Hudson. After the takeover by ACAP in April 1992 there was further confrontation between NATS and Hudson, who not only refused to top up NATS airline revenues but also asked that NATS pay rent for use of the airport control tower (the CAA weren't paying anything). It was an impasse and, as a result, NATS threatened to walk out, certain that this would bring Hudson to his senses or his knees.

This would be the first withdrawal of CAA/NATS facilities from any airport within recent memory and to outsiders it looked as if the airport would be left with a real problem — no air traffic control system, no air traffic. However, this facedown by NATS actually played into Hudson's hands. He wanted to control his own air traffic system, it was part of his airport business model, and it would save the airport money. Once again he was told it was too complicated to run, and could not be done. The CAA were demanding £1 million to continue serving the airport and a further £1 million for their equipment, including radar and instrument-landing systems. They owned it all and NATS were not prepared to lease. It was buy or nothing.

During protracted negotiations for the equipment during the next few months, Hudson discovered that various items could be bought brand new at a substantially-lower cost, with the added benefit of the manufacturers' guarantee and support. The company could also qualify for various grants to meet this cost, including a regional selective assistance grant of £150,000 from the Scottish Office, which would allow PIK to borrow half the approved cost of the new equipment at six per cent interest for five years and nine per cent for the other half. However, they would need to find staff for the new set-up.

Hudson said: "I always wanted to set up our own air traffic control system, and I had my own secret weapon: Tim Timlett." The former air traffic controller had served 19 years as a fighter pilot with the RAF before joining the Scottish Air Traffic Control Centre at Atlantic House, Prestwick, where he was for a time supervisor of all Scotland's airways. He retired from the CAA in 1985 but continued to work part-time and was a consultant with BAA in Kuala Lumpur for some years. In 1991 he received a call from Hudson. "The call came out of the blue," he said. "I didn't know who he was, but he said they were thinking of taking over the airport from BAA and revitalising Prestwick. Would I like to help?"

After some persuasion, Timlett took up the challenge to replace the NATS staff with PIK's own crew and set to work recruiting. All of the existing ATC staff had been offered jobs in other parts of the country, a move viewed by

Hudson as a ploy by CAA to stop their senior staff going to work for PIK. Similar tactics had been employed by NATS in other parts of the country, he said, to help protect its monopoly in this field. There were many difficulties in transferring CAA services over to an independent private service, especially in getting staff a validated rating through the CAA. Air traffic personnel were in short supply and it takes a long time to train them. Timlett got a lot of replies from foreigners and from experienced staff at other airports, but that brought its own problems. Although the controllers he recruited held their CAA ATC licences and were working at airports, they all had to be re-validated because they were changing airports.

This meant training in local procedures and geography and passing a CAA examination before being allowed to go solo. Engineers also had to satisfy the CAA of their competency to maintain the complex equipment. Fortunately, a number of recruits were granted dispensations due to their long experience, allowing them to work while going through their validation. These people had to go through an intensive ground school before they began so they knew the area's topography. Timlett chose the most suitable candidates and he set up the training course.

Strict regulations governing the work of air traffic controllers led to difficulties in maintaining a full 24-hour roster at Prestwick during the validation process. Shifts and working hours are also closely governed, and CAA officers can walk into any airport for a spot inspection at any time of the day or night to check equipment or documentation. If they thought the airport unsafe they could close it. Furthermore, airports are allowed their own air traffic control team only if the CAA agree they are competent. Timlett's team at Prestwick passed that test and on April 1 1993 took control of the tower. They started with four very experienced controllers, the rest were new, younger people still undergoing training. "It was a struggle to start with," said Timlett, "but we got there."

PIK had opened for business as proud owners of an airport which boasted two runways; the trouble was that part of the second, shorter, narrower runway was now covered in grass and home to a flock of sheep belonging to a neighbouring farmer. Grazing rights had been granted to the farmer because the full length of the second runway had not been essential to the operation of the airport under BAA management, nor to the flight testing of British Aerospace and the flying college.

In what was regarded as part of BAA's rundown of Prestwick in the 1980s, land which included part of the runway was gifted to Kyle and Carrick District Council to enable them to create a Freeport which, it was expected, would increase business activity around the airport. The council had won a long battle for Freeport status for Prestwick and were delighted to take up the opportunity to progress their plan. The development came just as fears were emerging about the future of the airport and the council were keen to repeat the success of a similar venture at Shannon Airport in Ireland, where a very successful Freeport allowed companies to bring, process and ship out goods without paying tax. So, in 1984, Freeport (Scotland) was born, with Ayr businessman Bill Barr as chairman of the board. BAA held a 17 per cent share in the Freeport company while other early shareholders were the council, (34 per cent) the Clydesdale Bank and Jim Moffat of AT Mays who, like the council, would later go on to be on the board of PIK Ltd.

However, the timing wasn't great for the new Freeport. Unfortunately for the council and the shareholders, regulations were changed around that time so that airports no longer needed Freeports for the easy movement of goods. In fact the Freeport was never developed to its full potential. This initial agreement in 1984 was valid for 25 years and an option gave the Freeport developers the right at any time to require BAA to provide a 99-year lease over some or all of the second runway and the taxiway. The option, for which nothing was paid, was perhaps meant to take effect immediately but it didn't. Also there was no obligation on the Freeport developers to actually accept a lease after exercising this option. Through the somewhat-convoluted agreement, BAA also retained the right to take back any part of the gift if it needed land for operational purposes, but only if the option had not been exercised and only after giving 12 months notice to the developers. What this in effect meant was that should BAA ever wish to regain the use of the second runway or any part of it, they would need to give the Freeport 12 months notice, during which time the developers could send a letter exercising their option over any piece of the runway, no matter how small, no matter where located. Then having done so, the developers would still have no obligation to ask for a lease. The Freeport had total control. Thus BAA gave away the future of the second runway for no commercial gain and with it BAA gave away any potential Prestwick might have had to compete with BAA's Heathrow as the international gateway to Europe.

The second runway happened to border Heathfield, on the outskirts of Ayr, an area long earmarked for development by numerous local councils. In 1984, when BAA decided to close the second runway it thereby effectively removed it as a development constraint affecting the 124-acre Heathfield property. This allowed BAA to begin looking at its development potential. Planners were engaged and discussions with the local planning authority proceeded on the basis that the "former second runway" would never be used again. In 1987, when BAA was privatised, the Heathfield property was part of the assets, passed on to Lynton Properties, the BAA's property division. The following year the original shareholders of the Freeport company amended the articles of the company so that each of the original shareholders would always be entitled to a directorship so long as they owned any shares. However the right to be a director was not extended to any future shareholders not named in the articles. A special and private club appeared to be materialising.

The same year, Kyle and Carrick District Council drew up a Heathfield Development Strategy based on the closure of the former second runway. During 1988 there was no action by the Freeport developers on their option and during that time BAA took back a small portion of the runway on three occasions to provide the BAe Flying College with a short facility — each time giving less than the requisite 12 months notice. No objections were raised, however. During the same year, BAA plc entered an agreement with a property and housing developer regarding their 241-acre Heathfield site. Applications were made and developments pursued by Wimpey and Betts. One plan was for housing, the other for a large retail development. The land was still owned by BAA but at this stage they preferred to have others carry out the development.

By summer 1990, BAA was aware that there could be interest in buying the airport to secure its future. And that July, after six years of silence, the Freeport sprung into action and exercised its option over a strip of the runway and a taxiway which bisected the land. This was done in such a way that the runway could not be used again for aviation purposes. However there was still no mention of a lease. Again in 1991 there was still no mention of a lease as the local ACAP consortium continued to work on their plan to rescue the airport. In early 1992 the structure and principles of the deal were agreed and Hudson asked BAA to ensure that the adjacent land would be sold to the new owners. In fact BAA had in the previous few months quietly sold off large parcels of land.

So on April 1, 1992, the new owners had an airport shorn of much its second runway and much of its adjacent land. Hudson had insisted, with George Younger's help, that BAA, as part of the transaction agree to sell its shares in the Freeport company to the new owners. At that point some of the other shareholders attempted to change the articles of the Freeport again, this time to prevent the transfer of the BAA shares to ACAP. However BAA voted against the move and Councillor Ian Welsh, avid airport supporter and by now the district council's majority leader, alerted by the airport's new owners, instructed the council chief executive to vote against and the motion failed to attract the necessary 75 per cent vote.

The new owners, PIK Ltd, now registered objections to the two large developments being planned for the Heathfield site, Bett's retail development along the main road and 300 houses by Wimpey, adjacent to the end of the runway. The airport owners subsequently met with economic development officials of the district council and withdrew objections to the retail development. Wimpey, meantime, submitted a new housing application.

However, there was still the thorny question of the use of the second runway. Both PIK and British Aerospace, when they had taken over ownership of the airport and the factory site, wanted the second runway in full operation for a number of reasons. First there was noise and safety: a neighbour whose house was only a mile from the end of the main runway was constantly disturbed by noise from training flights from the college, of which there could be more than 100 a day. In fact BAe and the flying college were inundated with noise complaints from Nigel Angus, a racehorse trainer. He had taken legal advice which had resulted in the circuit pattern for the trainee pilots being changed from a right hand to a left-hand one. But this in turn had led to safety concerns. With trainee pilots taking a left circuit pattern, they had to fly over the town of Prestwick or close to the sea. A pilot in difficulty would have no choice but to ditch in the sea or to look for an area of grass in Prestwick on which to land. There are few such grassy areas in the town so the full second runway gave a safer option for a forced landing. Although the second runway had been partially open, the fence penning in the sheep made such landings impossible.

Then there was the BAe Jetstream programme. The plant at this time was manufacturing both the Jetstream 31 and 41. With a fully-functioning second runway, the flight test programme could continue despite wind conditions. In fact, BAe's Allan MacDonald considered the second runway essential to his flight test and development programme. Matthew Hudson also considered that full use of the second runway was essential to the successful rebirth of the airport. Amongst other considerations it would provide an emergency landing facility in event of an engine malfunction or in other circumstances, say, if a plane blocked the main runway.

The law of averages, Hudson said, would dictate that sometime, somewhere an aircraft was going to block a runway due to an incident or accident, for any amount of time, from minutes to hours. Use of the entire second runway would also enable larger aircraft to take off from Prestwick regardless of wind direction. So, ignoring Freeport considerations, work to restore the full length of the second runway began in January 1993. Hudson advised the district council of the need to reopen the runway and gave a probable date of February 15. The plan was to have it up and running by March 5 1993, the date on which it was licensed for operation by the CAA. There followed a battle of wills between two groups who both claimed to have the best interests of the airport at heart and who came close to damaging it.

PIK wanted the runway operational, but first they had to get rid of the sheep. Legal action was begun to remove the grazing rights which had been granted to the farmer. That was successful and as the bulldozers moved in to clear the fence, work began on removing the grass and improving the runway surface. A trickier obstacle was the Freeport option over the ground. The Freeport board were not for budging. Not surprisingly, they were not overly pleased at the work being undertaken to clear the runway without their permission. They responded immediately and, at last, decided to take up their much-ignored lease option. At a board meeting in February 1993, a unanimous decision was taken, without discussion, to seek entry to the property and to build a new fence across the runway to replace the one taken down by Hudson. This, of course, would handicap the activities of trainee pilots from the flying school and would hold up BAe's Jetstream programme. It might also threaten jobs at the plant, though none of these issues seemed to concern the Freepost board.

Although that move perhaps came as no surprise, what did astonish PIK and BAe was that two of the board members who agreed to this move were representatives of Kyle and Carrick District Council, who were shareholders in PIK and had a seat on their board. PIK saw this as a deliberate ploy to inhibit the development of the airport and the situation became further complicated with Wimpey's plans to build houses on the periphery of the runway. Wimpey were now questioning the right of PIK to use the runway, claiming this would create a noise insulation problem for them.

George Younger, now with a peerage, having been elevated to the House of Lords after the 1992 May elections, stepped in to try to mollify matters with a letter to the district council, which was now Tory-led following the local elections. He wanted to clear past misunderstandings, he told Provost Gibson Macdonald, who was a council representative on the Freeport Board. He thought they should make a fresh start in view of the council's sizeable investment in the airport.[*]

Provost Macdonald said the Freeport board took the view that they had the legal option to stop the runway being opened. The council's view, he said, was that the Freeport had an asset and they were not going to roll over and say "You can have it for nothing." The Provost described Hudson as intransigent. "He needed the runway for his great dreams for the future of freight and the airport and he

---

[*] In 1995 the Thatcher government took the view councils could not be involved in airports. The statute covering the ownership of airports or shares in airports had existed for many years.

It had been ignored by the government on many occasions for major English airports. No one on the council knew of it and the auditors had passed the accounts for the council showing the shareholding and left the matter without comment. Later when the airport was becoming a commercial success the original b shares held by the council were to be converted to a shares and Matthew Hudson asked that the council get government permission from the Ministry of Aviation before share conversion. A single letter from the ministry giving exemption would have been sufficient to regularise the matter but this was not forthcoming

Dr Brian Mawhinney, Secretary of State of Transport told Kyle and Carrick District Council he was not willing to sanction the holding of shares in PIK Holdings. A department spokesman said at the time: "It is government policy to discourage local authorities from becoming involved in the running of airports and to leave it to the private sector. Indeed the Secretary of State is actively encouraging local authorities to divest themselves of any shareholding and as such was unwilling to allow Kyle and Carrick to continue its holding."

Said Councillor Gibson Macdonald. "It is a pity that there was no one with clout within the Tory government who could have obtained the letter."

The council which had made the whole deal possible and invested public money in buying the terminal from BAA to lease it back to PIK was forced to unwillingly sell its shares back to the company at cost – so it made no profit on the transaction to its eternal regret and annoyance.

was just going to take it. It was an asset we had and we don't give away assets."

In April 1993, BAe decided it was time to flex its considerable muscle, calling on Jonathan Walton to enter the fray by writing on behalf of the company to all the Freeport board members spelling out the position as BAe saw it. He emphasised their increased use of the re-opened runway as part of the Jetstream programme, its importance to the future development of the company and he questioned the motives behind the Freeport decision to put the fence back and virtually close the second runway. Walton wrote: "It was with considerable alarm that we learned of Freeport Scotland Ltd's decision to seek entry to a section of runway 03/21 in effect, it seems, attempting to undo all PIK Ltd have done to re-commission it." Without commenting on the legal aspects of the option, he added: "I want you to know that we have serious concerns about the motives behind the Freeport Scotland Ltd's board decision."

He could not see that the Freeport had any genuine need to extend its land holding — i.e. the second runway — pointing out that the Free Zone had in fact been reduced to 5.8 acres from the 32.9 acres originally designated in 1984. He reckoned the Freeport already had more than enough land to develop further and he warned that BAe would vigorously oppose any planning application or building consents made for the land. The letters, with slight variations, went to the chairman, Bill Barr, Provost Macdonald, and the chief executive of the Clydesdale Bank — this particular letter included a reminder that a third of the BAe staff banked with Clydesdale, including Allan MacDonald and that the BAe in Australia banked with the parent National Australia Bank.

Provost Macdonald was first to respond, saying he had thought the situation was a "wind-up" and that since the Freeport were made aware of Jetstream's concerns they had decided not to pursue the closure of the runway. He added, however, that the Freeport would be pursuing a commercial claim for the loss of the option against PIK Ltd. Any loss they would claim would be for lost rent that they might have obtained in the next 100 years for the land in question. "PIK is a private company," he said, "and Mr Hudson should not be able to ride roughshod over other private companies like the Freeport." The council, he said, would be prepared to make other land available to the Freeport should it wish to expand. He claimed that the Freeport had been trying to secure discussions with PIK for a year over the subject but had met with no response, which had led them to pursue the issue in the way they had. The decision to reinstate the fence was an effort to bring PIK to the negotiating table, claimed Provost Macdonald

Meantime, Hudson, in solicitor mode and with Walton's support, was questioning the validity of the Freeport option. He argued there was no need for the Freeport to have additional land and that the runway was not part of the designated Free Zone as determined by a 1991 redesignation of the Freeport area. He also claimed that outline planning consent for Freeport use had lapsed and pointed out that the Freeport had paid nothing for the option, since it was a gift from BAA who had, he said, embarked some years previously on a concerted campaign to dismantle Prestwick Airport due to their preference to develop Glasgow.

Although council representatives were responding to the situation, there was as yet no official response from Freeport Scotland Ltd and their chairman Bill Barr. Then, in May, BAe and PIK learned of a plan to institute legal proceedings in order to obtain a Decree of Declarator of a heritable right over the land in question. Walton wrote to the Freeport on behalf of BAe: "If it is Freeport Scotland's intention to use a Decree of Declarator as leverage to exact a commercial settlement from PIK Ltd, we would strongly protest at part of an important local and national asset and essential operational facility used by British Aerospace, the largest employer in the area, being used in this way. The risk of closure that would continue to hang over the runway if no settlement could be reached would be totally unacceptable to us."

He hoped the council could exert its influence to find a settlement. In the end, PIK exercised the company's right to acquire the shareholding of BAA in the Freeport Company which, combined with the shares owned by the district council, amounted to 51 per cent of the issued share capital. The issue finally was submitted to counsel, who opined in agreement with PIK's legal position that the Freeport had no property claim to the second runway.

Cargo

Boeing 747-200

YO

PIK

Chapter 9
Freightliner
Freightliner

D EVELOPING the freight business was a priority for Matthew Hudson: build up freight first, make the airport profitable and the passengers would follow. But in the middle of March 1992, just a fortnight before PIK were due to take over the airport, a phone call looked like putting that course in jeopardy. It was David Mullen, Fedex regional manager based at Prestwick and a Prestwick campaigner, speaking from the FedEx HQ in Memphis, Tennessee, saying he had information that FedEx, operators of the airport's only flights, were planning to pull out. He told Hudson the airport was "not on the board for May". It was a bolt from the blue. If true, Prestwick was at risk of losing its last shred of aviation credibility. Not only would it be a terminal with no passengers, now it would have no planes, either.

Until that point, FedEx had been great supporters of Prestwick. Hudson had planned on forming a service partnership with FedEx to provide the logistically-based freight services that Silicon Glen needed so that the Scottish PC manufacturers could compete with far east plants in Singapore, Korea and Hong Kong. Hudson had no option. He travelled, uninvited, to Memphis and parked himself outside the office of Fred Smith, the founder and CEO of FedEx, until he was granted a meeting.

Smith and Hudson were alike in many ways: both were hands-on managers directing every facet of corporate strategy. They spoke the same language and got on well together. Smith had started his express transport business in 1971 after leaving the military, where he had served two tours of duty in Vietnam with the Marine Corps. He raised $80 million to launch Federal Express, beginning modestly with small packages and documents. In the first two years the venture lost $27 million and Smith lost all of his investors' money, but he renegotiated loans and kept his company afloat. By 1997 the company was worth $16 billion, employed 170,000 and was shipping goods all round the world, from contact lenses to auto parts. As part of Hudson's strategy to attract freight, he had wanted Fred Smith to become involved.

After intense negotiation, and although he emerged with an undertaking from Smith that the company would take a 10 per cent share in PIK, Hudson was no further forward in establishing whether his tip-off that FedEx were preparing to pull out from May was correct. What was he to do? Should he hope the information was wrong, hope that Smith would over-rule his operating team, or should he put the takeover into jeopardy by being upfront about the possibility of losing FedEx, risking a negative reaction from BAe? He talked the issue over with Bill Miller and both came to the same conclusion: they felt public knowledge would be risky at this late stage and could put the whole deal in jeopardy. So Hudson quietly passed the information to the other investors and they stayed silent,

Previous page: At Prestwick, cargo was crucial to the airport's survival in the days after the successful buyout by the PIK group *Photograph courtesy of Phil Toman*

while keeping their fingers crossed.

David Mullin had recently become Fed-Ex regional manager for Scotland and Northern Ireland, after a long and happy association with the airport. Throughout the 1980s, he had been a major player in the battle to keep Prestwick flying as regional manager Scotland and Northern Ireland for Flying Tigers, the largest cargo carriers in the world. His concern was that the closure of the airport would drive all the freight flights south of the border. There was no likelihood of major operators such as Flying Tigers going to Glasgow — the runway was too short. "My argument throughout the campaign was that the closure of Prestwick would destroy freighter operations in Scotland and freighter operations were critical to the manufacturing base and supported jobs in Scotland. I also argued that Prestwick, labelled 'remote' by the media was no more remote than any other major airport. No matter where an airport is situated it will always be remote from somewhere. Glasgow is remote to the western Highlands just as Swansea is remote to the main transatlantic airports in London. Prestwick was only remote when it became a political issue."

Hudson was concerned that during this campaign plenty of media exposure was being given to airlines leaving Prestwick but no one had bothered reporting that the largest air freight carriers in the world had set up successfully at the Ayrshire airport. Freight did not have the glamour of the big passenger carriers, but freight had played a big part in the success of Prestwick Airport through the 1970s and while passenger numbers fell in the 1980s the freight business remained strong.

By 1990, while the airport was struggling to stay open, Flying Tigers was taken over by FedEx, with David Mullin continuing in his post, and by then they were the airport's main source of income. He recalls his first, crucial meeting with the "dynamic and aggressive" Matthew Hudson. "He certainly didn't go out to win friends. He was quite clear that it was his job to champion the airport and if you weren't part of the solution, then you were part of his problem. But the argument in his favour was that he did not have time to waste winning reluctant people over."

Mullin was a key man for Hudson to get on side as the face of FedEx in Scotland and Hudson explained his plans to develop the airport. Mullin, for his part, said: "FedEx cannot save the airport, but we can buy you time." In other words he was prepared to do his bit to keep FedEx coming into Prestwick while Hudson worked to expand the freight operations. Hudson knew Mullin had great personal loyalty to his boss, Fred Smith, and that he would apply the maximum effort to generate the considerable revenue required to keep the FedEx operation viable and to keep them coming to Prestwick.

It became clear that the middle management team in Memphis was determined to pull out of Prestwick, but with the takeover date looming and negotiations at a critical stage, Hudson couldn't fly back to Memphis. There was still too much to do.

But early in April, Hudson *was* back in Memphis and arranged to meet up with Fred Smith for dinner. Hudson explained the lift, load and revenue reports being given to Smith, on which the anti-Prestwick sentiment within FedEx was based, were misleading. They showed Prestwick without any inbound revenue, because the computer system only had a UK code and that all revenue was allocated to London. Hudson also worked on convincing Smith that he could guarantee the fastest turnaround times of any airport in the world. His team were good, he said. "To take freight we needed two things, well-trained, highly-motivated men and excellent, well-maintained, reliable ramp equipment. We were very, very good on the ramp. Everybody was motivated and tried really hard. We were also very safe since at least one of the large Crash and Fire trucks was parked right behind the aircraft and at least 50% of the ramp workers were also members of the Crash and Fire Rescue Service," said Hudson. Fred Smith listened: FedEx stayed.

That success was pivotal to Hudson's business plan to establish the financial viability of the airport via freight, allowing him to think about plans to go after passengers and bring low cost air fares for Scotland.

Bill Miller was also championing the freight case for Prestwick and recalls sensing a change in the air within the Scottish business community. As vice chairman of the Scottish CBI and the Scottish Council for Development and Industry he had never missed an opportunity to plead Prestwick's case: "In fact it almost became a joke," he said. "Every time I stood up at a meeting they knew I would be banging on about Prestwick." But he knew he had to get the freight message over.

Eventually he managed his own little coup. At his instigation, the Scottish CBI and the Scottish Council for Development and Industry agreed to come together in Glasgow to discuss air freight — quite an achievement in that these two organisations were not natural bedfellows; one was an employers' association while the other was an all-sector organisation which included trades union members. "I think there was a bit of a guilt complex," said Miller, "because the business community had been vocal in supporting Glasgow in the Open Skies battle." Lord Younger was the main speaker and the conference marked a turning point in the Scottish business community supporting Prestwick.

One year on, Hudson's freight strategy was working. From preliminary research he was targeting help from the electronics industry while Miller was able to introduce Hudson to MDs and chief executives of some of the major players in the sector. Hudson remembers: "They didn't know anything about the logistics of moving freight. Basically, the freight decisions were made by whoever ran the shipping dock and his decisions could be based on whichever freight forwarder gave him the biggest bottle of whisky at Christmas."

The freight forwarders were getting all the business and their own 'business' was to consolidate. The company bosses thought the freight forwarder was their

Hugh Lang and former provost of Kyle and Carrick, Gibson Macdonald, mark the launch of Direct Holiday flights from Prestwick *Photo courtesy of Phil Toman*

agent who was out there getting them the best rates and the best shipping arrangements. "That's not what they were doing," said Hudson. He told the MDs that their forwarders were probably getting the cheapest rate but it wasn't the best service for the rate as the forwarders sold the lift capacity to the shippers for whatever they could get, then purchased the cheapest lift possible — belly freight. Belly freight was goods on passenger aircraft. This was cheap to buy from the passenger airlines who had belly space going empty, but it was not the best method to get the shippers' goods from A to B reliably and quickly. Twenty four hours from Glasgow to Singapore by FedEx might be eight days by belly and their goods would bounce through four, five, even six airports — then it might arrive damaged through repeated rehandling. Often goods did not arrive at all, having been stolen en route.

Hudson gradually began to educate the MDs in the vagaries of logistics, telling them: "Freight is dedicated first-class travel for your high-value, time-sensitive goods."

He confirmed to these companies that their freight was almost certainly going cargo, the cheapest but also the slowest route. Getting the companies to understand this suited Hudson's purpose and put him in the position of being able to offer the most efficient freight service around, operated solely by the airport staff, cutting out the middle men — but this all depended on being able to attract more carriers. "No one was listening to us at the start," said Hudson. "They would say: 'Hey are you guys still open?' They didn't know about us. BAA had done a good job saying we were silly amateurs."

By this time Hudson had been running almost a one-man band — the original PIK operating company MD Mike Dooley had left shortly after the takeover, and some months later he was replaced as managing director by Paddy Healey, a friend of Hudson and a friend of the airport. Healey had been commanding officer of the neighbouring HMS Gannet, a tenant of the airport. In June 1993, as the airport was stabilising and the freight business was growing, Hudson was looking round to develop it commercially to the next level and needed someone to take over responsibility for freight. After running advertisements locally and throughout Scotland and doing all of his own interviewing, he took on a young local man, Hugh Lang, who was just completing his MBA at Strathclyde University after a stint as a geologist on a rig in the Gulf of Mexico.

Lang recalls: "I had just finished all my MBA work but hadn't yet graduated and I was looking for a job that was different. I saw the advertisement and applied for the airport job on spec. After the interview I was speaking to Matthew about equipment and said I had a computer. When he hired me he asked that I arrive on my first day in my new job with my own computer and printer. That was how costs were kept down. I sometimes wonder if it was the fact that I had a computer that got me the job!"

Hudson quickly set about teaching Lang the ins and outs of the freight business and in March 1994 they had their first major success when they won over the giant carrier Cargolux, converting a refuelling stop into a full freight service. This brought in their first 747 freighter. While the Cargolux refuelling deal was in operation, Lang discovered that it was bound for Luxembourg, where freight load was unloaded before being trucked back to Britain by road. Lang offered Cargolux the opportunity to unload at Prestwick instead of continuing to Luxembourg — but a maze of red tape prevented the freight operators from taking it up.

It took a visit by Hudson and Lang to the Ministry of Transport in London and six months of negotiation before the path was cleared for Cargolux to fly into Prestwick — and then the floodgates were opened. Within months, they had Lufthansa flying in from Houston, Texas, and the freight business started to seriously build up. Prestwick became a prime airport for freight handling in terms of quality and service. They were top of the range and convinced customers they had an operation that suited their needs and, in turn, the customers gave the airport their support. Eventually, Prestwick was handling more wide-bodied freighters than all the London airports combined.

There was a huge demand for priority products and fast-moving freight plus, of course, reliability and only Prestwick had the will and the skill at that time to meet the strict service needs. The freight was mostly electronic but the airport also handled bigger loads, including engines for Caledonian Airmotive. They also carried livestock, which led to one of the airport's most controversial episodes when Hudson agreed to the transportation by air of British veal calves into Europe in December 1994, when Compassion in World Farming had picketed docks all over the country and had succeeded in getting a ban on the export of live animals by channel ferries.

Hudson said: "The male calves were unwanted by the dairy farmers and would either be killed shortly after birth and buried in pits on the farms or could be transported to Europe for fattening in pens, then slaughtered and sold as veal. They came from farms in England, Ireland and Scotland and had been transported to Europe for years in the holds of small cargo ships. Because of pickets and some rioting at the docks in England, we were asked if we would accept air freight operations, since all of the English airports with large enough runways had refused. I agreed: we were in business and it was good business."

He regarded the venture as a way to do a good job for his employees and a better job for the veal calves. He was convinced he was right both morally and ethically in handling the livestock. He said: "The poor little calves were better off in the belly of a freight aeroplane for an hour or two than in the hold of a ship for what might be several days. Before we came along they had been put in a ship where they were banged about on the waves. It must have been terrible for them. Compared to that, flying was quick and easy, a relative luxury. I told the animal rights campaigners that the calves were going to go anyway and if they said the animals couldn't go by plane, then they were condemning them to go by ship. It seemed to me I was the one who was caring about the animals, not them. They didn't like that, but it was true."

He also tried to claim that legally the airport was not allowed to refuse to fly the animals; it would be a breach of CAA guidelines. However, the CAA disagreed with Hudson. They claimed they would not be in breach and he was forced into holding a two-week review of the decision to fly the animals. Then, in a bizarre press conference-cum-discussion, and after a last-minute change of venue because of protestors gathering outside with placards, Hudson declared the airport was going ahead with the flights, saying he had a moral responsibility to the animals, the surplus 500,000 veal calves produced in the country each year.

In an attempt at damage limitation, Hudson had invited welfare groups to the press conference along with a veterinary advisor from the Meat and Livestock Commission and tried to placate the campaigners by suggesting the creation of a not-for-profit foundation to raise money for action on the wider issues, including genetic research for the production of female dairy calves only, establishing a better system of monitoring continental rearing facililties, and lobbying the European Community for regulations to upgrade animal rearing standards to those of Britain and Spain.

He detailed proposals for a voluntary Code of Practice for all UK airports governing the transport of calves, including minimum resting and feeding times and a clause that no airport should profit from the transportation of the calves. The cargo handling fee, he suggested, could go to the non-profit foundation. The airport even took out full-page adverts in national newspapers justifying their decision, explaining that flying was more "welfare friendly" and that any fees involved would be donated to animal welfare. The three animal groups — Compassion in World Farming, Animal Concern and Advocates for Animals — were not impressed. They were furious at the decision to proceed with the flights and threatened to mount an intensive campaign to persuade people and businesses not to fly from the airport.

"The media loved it of course," said Hudson. But events turned serious when he started to receive threats to his safety. He said: "Some crazies got involved. I had made it clear through the media that this was my decision and mine alone, so I received a couple of death threats. Special Branch were called in and we were warned to check our cars, which could be targeted. The police would come and check under my car and I was advised to do the same before driving it."

Although Hudson claimed sole responsibility for the decision, Special Branch advised other members of staff to be careful, particularly when opening mail. "All these organisations have extremists," said Sandra Clarkson, Hudson's PA for six years. "It was quite a frightening time." Still convinced he was doing the right thing, Hudson spoke to the farmers who were exporting the calves and went into great detail as to how best to transport the animals; he went to Brussels to speak to commissioners so he knew all about the business from calf to end product. He even set up pens at the airport so the calves got rest, food, water and relaxation.

None of this appeased the animal rights activists, however, who picketed the airport and Hudson was shouted down during a debate on TV. Eventually, shipping by sea resumed and the flights stopped.

NOW it was time to bring passengers back to Prestwick; the new owners had been operating the airport for a year and the freight strategy was taking off. It was time to put bums on seats. Hudson's plan was to build an entirely new passenger business while solving the problem of the exorbitant cost of passenger access to and from Scotland. Scottish passengers were regularly incensed to find their holidays abroad cost more than those of their counterparts south of the border. Hudson knew there had been some dissent in the local community when he had focused his efforts on freight immediately after taking over the airport; to most people an airport was about passengers. At that time, however, Hudson believed what Scotland needed was logistically-effective freight services so that the critical Scottish electronics industry could ensure its survival through access to the global marketplace. Freight had been his first goal, but now he was going after people, a whole new class of passengers, those who didn't normally travel by air, and to do that he knew Glasgow Prestwick, as it was now called, had to be able to offer something Glasgow Abbotsinch Airport (as he insisted on calling it) didn't have. That, he decided, was easy and inexpensive access for everyone, car owner or not.

The Glasgow Prestwick name change had been a tricky decision. Hudson was well aware of the local sensitivities and, of course, the long battle between the two airports over transatlantic flights, but being a realist he also knew that the name Glasgow was better known worldwide than Prestwick. It was part of the pilots' airport call sign and more importantly it would annoy the hell out of the BAA Scotland management. He knew they called Prestwick a Mickey Mouse operation — in fact he proudly wore a Mickey Mouse watch he had picked up in Florida as a mark of defiance — and he was on a mission to prove them wrong. Also London had London Heathrow and London Gatwick, so why should Glasgow not have two airports — Prestwick and Abbotsinch?

Glasgow Airport, without a direct rail link, could be difficult to reach and passengers would get frustrated as they were stuck in traffic jams through the city centre trying to get on to the M8 approach to the airport. Passengers who chose to go by rail had to take the train from Glasgow and disembark at the nearby town of Paisley and then opt for a taxi or the airport bus link for the final three miles or so to the airport, all of which added time and uncertainty to the journey. Prestwick had for too long been perceived as being too far away, an impression skilfully nurtured during the Gateway status campaign, and Hudson now set out to change that.

"What I looked at was not the travel time, but the process time," said Hudson. "Nobody ever looks at that. Process time is defined as from the time you leave your front door until the time your bum is on the seat in the plane. What is the total time you need? That is the process time. I used to tell people, yes it is true we are further away, but you don't get traffic jams once you get out of Glasgow. You may have to drive an extra 25 minutes but once you get here, it is different. From the moment you arrive on our airport property until your bum is on the seat on the plane, you are saving time, a lot of time, at Prestwick. So your total process time is shorter, partly because it is much more predictable, so you don't need to allow the extra 30/45/60 minutes 'just in case'."

Hudson knew Prestwick needed a railway halt of its own, linked to the terminal, the ticket desks and departure/arrival hall. The main Ayr-to-Glasgow line ran alongside the airport. There had been talk for years about building a railway station at the airport and in fact there had been provision for a linked access from the rail line included in the design of the terminal building in the 1960s. There had never seemed to be the money, the interest or the enthusiasm for such a massive project. Until now. By early 1993 Hudson was instructing a design team and plans for the rail halt were being drawn up. However, this was going to take time, something Hudson did not have if he wanted to get the passengers back on planes. They would need permits, they would need to find financing, there would be construction delays; it would be a difficult and expensive job due to the need to make rail and road closures. As these were going to take a considerable time to complete,.

In the meantime, Hudson decided to offer potential passengers a deal they could not refuse: free travel to Prestwick Town station from any part of Scotland, by train or coach. It was a master stroke.

Summer holiday charter companies were beginning to take an interest in what Prestwick could offer and he knew free rail travel would be an added attraction, for passengers and the travel companies. So in February 1993, after some serious negotiating, he set up a special ticketing deal with the Strathclyde Passenger Transport Executive and ScotRail, offering free travel by train or bus to and from any part of Scotland to the airport for passengers flying into or out of Prestwick. The deal was complex in creation, achievement and operation but simple for the public to use. PIK would pay SPTE £1.50 for every passenger travelling. Fifty pence of that would go to ScotRail and, in return, each passenger would get a voucher covering the return journey from their home to the airport. The passengers got their vouchers by presenting their air ticket at the rail or bus station. The scheme started on April 1, 1993, a by now familiar and favourite date for PIK, and continued until December, 1994, until the privatisation of the rail network put an end to the arrangement.

August 1993 saw the launch of a £100,000 multi-media marketing campaign designed to promote the holiday programme for 1994 and to place PIK firmly in the Scottish travel market. Five tour operators were announced as having committed to the 1994 programme: Direct Holidays, Inspirations Holidays, Style, Med Choice and The Club. A winter programme of flights to Florida was also announced around the same time, to start on November 23 that year. The media campaign focused on Prestwick's advantages over Glasgow — cheaper holidays, by at least £15 a head; car parking would only be £5 a week; there was the free rail/bus travel, of course, and a maximum 10-minute check-in. Once checked in the passengers then had more time to enjoy the cheapest duty-free in Scotland.

The marketing campaign was followed by the launch of a road show taking the Prestwick International concept to the furthermost parts of the country, emphasising the benefits of flying from the Ayrshire airport. The cherry on the cake was the promise of a new rail station by the following June, which was going to be integrated into the airport's concourse and reached by a covered walkway over the road. The plan was coming together.

When Hudson first floated the idea of a rail halt at the airport he approached ScotRail, the main operators for Scotland. They replied that they did not build rail stations and even if they did consider it, it would take five years to do a market study and that would probably say the airport couldn't afford it. Even if the market study didn't kill the idea, they said, it would take several years to fund it, then a further five years to design it and then several years to build it. "That's fine," Hudson told them. "But I need it now, so I'll build my own." He started another of his detailed self-teaching research projects, this time to find out how rail stations were built and he had help here from fellow director and friend Sir David McNee, whose father had worked for the railway. He still had

Passengers board an Air Colombus aircraft on the first charter flight from Prestwick. Right: the new owners began to aggressively market the airport to a hitherto untapped market: holidaymakers.

Photograph courtesy of Phil Toman

a number of useful contacts and introduced Hudson to the famously-gruff Scottish rail union leader Jimmy Knapp.

Despite their ideological differences, the entrepreneur and the firebrand trade unionist hit it off immediately, Knapp recognising that Hudson was serious and that his plan would benefit the railway in Scotland. Hudson said: "I need your help, will you tell me how I can do this?" He told the union leader about the free rail travel offer and how it would help bring passengers back to Prestwick, which was of particular interested to Knapp, as he hailed from nearby Kilmarnock. Hudson told him: "I need your help to persuade the executives of ScotRail to work with me. They've got to want to make this work but right now all they are doing is telling me all sorts of reasons why it won't work."

Hudson recalled: "There was a great reluctance on the part of ScotRail for this scheme to see the light of day so with Jimmy as my main fellow plotter I set out to invigorate and convert ScotRail. Eventually we won them over but it was hard going. But Jimmy Knapp was the key. If he hadn't supported me I don't know what I would have done."

The cost of the planned station and skywalk linking it to the main terminal building was estimated at around £2 million. Who would pay for it? Again the district council was among the first to offer support with a Scottish Office-approved contribution of £400,000. Strathclyde Regional Council likewise gave £375,000 with a further £367,000 coming from the EEC and Enterprise Ayrshire handing over £426,000. PIK's contribution was £556,000. Management contractors Tarmac Construction started on site on Monday, November 29, 1993, and to mark the occasion, PIK hosted a special turf-cutting ceremony with Councillor Malcolm Waugh, chair of the Roads and Transportation Committee of Strathclyde Region, officiating. Guests included representatives of all the funding groups. Hudson told them: "The lack of a dedicated rail station for Prestwick International has long been viewed as the airport's main disadvantage for passengers. The new £2 million rail station and skywalk will further strengthen our position as Scotland's most user-friendly airport, especially for vacation travellers including the all-important tourists."

One of the guests at the ceremony was Graham Shaw of Enterprise Ayrshire, who had been seconded to work with Hudson and initially had helped with the emerging business plan and the build-up of the freight infrastructure at the airport. Enterprise Ayrshire were interested in how a successful airport could contribute to the economic development of Ayrshire and Scotland. To Hudson, Enterprise Ayrshire were the obvious people to help with the rail halt project and initially they contributed by paying the salary of the project manager. But putting money upfront was not going to be so straightforward because of red tape. In the early 1990s if Enterprise Ayrshire wanted cash for a project they had to go through a huge appraisal system. First they had to estimate the demand, and this posed a problem as far as the rail halt was concerned. There were no passengers flying from Prestwick in 1993 so how could they justify a rail halt for non-existent travellers? Graham Shaw and his team opted for a statistical technique known as Stated Preference, which was centred on the idea: If there was a rail station there, would you use it?

Graham said: "We employed a London-based company who sent out four or five focus groups all over Scotland, pulling in a variety of people, and we managed to come up with a figure which was quite revolutionary at the time. Figures from the Stated Preference study said that if there was a rail station there 12 per cent of passengers would use it — much higher than the accepted norm."

They completed the paperwork, submitted it and sat back to await the challenges — after all, they were saying that here was an airport with no passengers but IF it had a rail halt, 12 per cent of these non-existent passengers would use it — double the expected figure for conventional airport-related rail usage in Europe. There were no airport rail stations in Great Britain at the time. Somehow, Enterprise Ayrshire managed to get their report accepted and their funding for the project was approved. The true significance of the value of the idea was seen by 2005 when 30 per cent of the almost two million passengers were using the rail halt, making it an unparalleled success story. No pie in the sky here.

"We were proved right," said Shaw, "but in all honesty I don't know how we got it accepted. We didn't really know what we were doing — we were flying by the seat of our pants."

Next problem for Enterprise Ayrshire was how to use their money. By their constitution they could not invest in transport infrastructure such as a railway station and for a time it looked as if all their hard work was going to come to nothing. Then Shaw realised the cash they were putting in could pay for the bridge over the highway, with the justification that it was providing access between two pieces of infrastructure. "To this day I don't know how or why they approved it but they did," laughed Shaw. "We were the proud contributors to this piece of metal going across the road."

The first section of the overhead walkway was lowered into place in June 13, 1994, in time for the station hopefully opening the following month. That, too, was not without its troubles as the crane operator employed to do the job had not operated such a large piece of equipment before and ran into trouble. He said the job would have to be delayed, but the PIK team had only the hours between midnight and 6am to complete the job before the mainline trains started running again. The job had to be completed there and then.

It was nail-biting stuff," said PIK director Bill Miller, who remembers standing with Hudson in the early hours watching the bridge being lowered. "Eventually we persuaded him to proceed and the bridge was lowered successfully, but it was a close-run thing."

The station was finally open to passengers on September 5, 1994. It was three months late — but it was open.

However this success was blighted on two counts with PIK taking legal action against the company who designed and constructed the station and overbridge — Scott, Wilson and Kilpatrick. PIK cited design and construction faults which led to the three-month delay in opening the station and additional costs. They sued them for £1,245,675. There was also a dispute with ScotRail who initially said they would need to charge PIK about £50,000 for "possessions, approvals and consultations." Their final bill was £250,000 — described by Hudson as "a travesty."

The Prestwick Airport station remains to this day the only privately-owned rail halt in Scotland.

PIK

Chapter 10

Fighting Talk

MATTHEW Hudson soon acquired the reputation for taking no prisoners in his business dealings. Being Canadian, a barrister and solicitor and a self-made, successful entrepreneur worth millions, he was not daunted by authority or position and was happy to tackle every issue head-on, regardless of whom he was dealing with. So he was not afraid, as many might have been, to face up to the might of the Ministry of Defence. The four main commercial planks of Hudson's pre-acquisition business plan were freight and logistics; charter passengers; low-cost; and property income.

When PIK took over Prestwick Airport the main initial income came from rents, and that included the naval base HMS Gannet on the neighbouring air station. It was formerly occupied by the United States Air Force from a few years after WWII into the late 1960s. HMS Gannet was home to 350 naval personnel and 11 Sea King helicopters. It was perhaps best known for its around-the-clock search and rescue cover but its first responsibility was as a forward base for anti-submarine operations, the nuclear subs going up and down the Firth of Clyde from their base at Faslane.

Income for the airport, the owners of the base, came from two sources: airfield and air traffic control fees generated by military flights and ground rental for two sites, one used for housing and the other for operational purposes. Hudson had assumed prior to getting sight of the leases — BAA made them available only in March 1992, months after PIK had agreed to buy the airport — that the property management regime of BAA, being run from London, would be overtaken by apathy. And he was right. When the time came for the MOD rents to be reviewed in November 1992, some seven months after PIK took ownership of the airport, Hudson decided they were far too low and brought in a local firm of chartered surveyors, Bell-Ingram, to conduct an inspection of the MOD "domestic" property and come up with an open market rental valuation. Taking into consideration the size, nature and location of the property John Cowan, a director of the company, said he considered a fair rental would be £360,000 a year. Under the same lease with BAA, the MOD had been paying £18,000. The operational site rent had been £110,000. Hudson's valuer felt that figure should have been £475,000.

"As you can imagine, some rockets went up at HMS Gannet and MOD London when we issued these figures," said Hudson. "They threatened to close the place down rather than pay a fair market price." However, Hudson reckoned there was no way they were going to close Gannet at that time and he thought they should pay the market price for their sites, just as it said in the leases, which had been negotiated between the MOD and the British Airports Authority. "Simply because BAA had

Previous page: **A row over landing fees reached the Court of Session in Edinburgh when the Ministry of Defence sought an interdict to prevent Matthew Hudson from grounding all aircraft at HMS Gannet, including the fleet of Royal Naval Sea King helicopters.** *Photograph courtesy of dtimages@hotmail.co.uk*

not administered their leases carefully was no reason for PIK to be profligate," said Hudson, who was also looking to increase the landing and ATC charges for the Sea King helicopters and other military traffic, charges which he also considered were too low during the BAA/CAA regimes.

While these disputes were ongoing, much to the MOD's embarrassment, Hudson discovered that the ministry had installed wiring at the naval air station that avoided the electricity meter, which meant that for years the navy had been using electricity belonging to the airport, electricity which the MOD did not pay for. However, faced with Hudson's demands, the MOD stubbornly stuck to their guns and insisted that notwithstanding the language of the leases, the previous arrangements with BAA over the years (rents and landing fees) and the CAA (ATC fees) should remain in place and that the rents and fees being sought by the new owners should not apply.

Hudson's view was that the MOD owed PIK Ltd around £100,000 for landing and navigation fees, but the Ministry of Defence were not listening, so he decided a touch of direct action was needed and he moved to ground all military aircraft at HMS Gannet. He also claimed right of lien (retaining possession of another's property pending the settling of a debt) over the aircraft which would give PIK the right to sell, remove or otherwise dispose of the craft, parts and accessories to satisfy the debt. On March 15, PIK wrote to lawyers acting for the Defence Secretary, Malcolm Rifkind — a former Secretary of State for Scotland — threatening that if the disputed rent was not paid by the end of the month that no further flying would be allowed, apart from the search-and-rescue services. The letter also talked of the intransigence of the Defence Secretary over the issue. Action then moved to the Court of Session in Edinburgh where the Ministry of Defence sought an interdict to prevent Hudson from virtually shutting down Gannet operations.

Raymond Doherty, counsel for the Lord Advocate representing the Ministry of Defence, told Lord Kirkwood that aircraft operating from HMS Gannet played an important part in the strategic defence of the UK and that they formed an important part of the protection given to operations at Faslane. Doherty told the judge that the Defence Secretary disputed the level of fees claimed by PIK and maintained that charges previously payable to BAA before PIK took over in 1992 were still operative. He also argued that the lien claimed over the aircraft by PIK was not enforceable over Crown property. He said the Defence Secretary had offered to deposit £100,000 in a joint account until the dispute was resolved but that PIK was still trying to enforce its rights. He pointed out that even if the court granted an interdict banning seizure of the aircraft, PIK could still pursue its claim for the money through the normal legal channels. If the company threat were not removed by a court order then the Defence Secretary would have to give immediate consideration to removing aircraft to another site. Lord Kirkwood granted an interdict banning PIK from attempting to detain any helicopters or aircraft at HMS Gannet and from selling, removing destroying or disposing of them or from obstructing the free movement of aircraft. PIK were not represented in court.

Paddy Healey, the new MD of the airport, and ironically former commanding officer at HMS Gannet, said he was sorry the issue could not have been resolved without going to court. Councillor Ian Welsh, by now a director on the PIK board in his own right, was a bit more forthright, saying it was "an outrage" that a small company trying to make its way in a difficult commercial world should be held to ransom by an arm of the British government. He said at the time: "Perhaps Malcolm Rifkind would like to have a look at this one and tell people to pay their bills before another important Scottish asset is put under threat."

The battle for rent and fee increases was to continue for almost three years and Hudson had to call on the influence of the PIK Group chairman, Lord Younger, and the new local Tory MP, Phil Gallie, to arrange meetings with two successive Ministers of the Defence. Meanwhile, Hudson told the MOD that he regarded the airport's working capital as being held hostage by the ministry's intransigence in the matter, and there was also the further question of the missing electricity money. Finally, in order to break the log-jam, he suggested a novel way forward to Nick Gurr of the Ministry of Defence at a meeting in London. Since the MOD solicitors had a different interpretation of the lease from Hudson, he proposed that a valuation expert be appointed by both sides and that the expert be asked to produce two valuations under each lease, one according to the MOD interpretation and one according to PIK's. He gave further comfort to the MOD by proposing that they could pre-select a shortlist of three valuers and that he would choose one of them to be the agreed expert. Both sides would then make submissions to the expert. The MOD agreed with this plan, since the agreed expert would be one selected by the MOD and one who could have worked for the MOD before and might do so again. On his side, Hudson took the gamble of finding an independent professional from amongst the three MOD choices.

As a result of this process the operations site was valued by the agreed expert at £386,000 (MOD interpretation) and £475,000 (PIK interpretation). Moreover, arrears and interest under the MOD interpretation were assessed at £550,000. The domestic site was valued at £176,000 (MOD) and £298,000 (PIK). Moreover, arrears and interest under the MOD interpretation were assessed at £350,000. So, based on the MOD's own interpretation of the leases, the annual rentals went from £128,000 to £562,000 and arrears of £900,000 were paid. This still left £211,000 of annual rentals "in play" under Hudson's interpretation of the leases but he would need to sue the MOD to get them.

Hudson told Nick Gurr in December 1995 that the delaying tactics of the MOD had severely affected the business of Prestwick Airport in that he had been forced to limit the summer charter programme because of a lack of working capital caused by the MOD arrears and lack of electricity payments. He added: "Although small, we are not without expertise in matters commercial and legal. We have been even-handed and as the results to date prove, restrained throughout this lengthy process which began three years ago." He warned he was not prepared to be "restrained" for much longer, adding that he was prepared to take legal action against the MOD and that he would be looking for a considerable sum in compensation for loss of other income during the three years of dispute. He also accused the MOD of bullying tactics in relation to flying services, landings and ATC.

A new flying agreement was eventually reached with the navy which would operate through to March 31, 1997. These agreements included a special night flying fee to compensate the airport for Fire and Crash Rescue Cover (minimum £75,000, maximum £125,000 annually) and arrears of approximately £225,000 were paid. Further, the navy agreed to be treated for operational and financial purposes like any other airline but with a 35 per cent discount, terminating the hotch-potch of rates agreed with BAA and bringing in another £30,000-£35,000 annually.

Thus, prior to any recourse to the courts or solicitors, Hudson had improved the annual yield from the MOD by some £620,000, plus one-time payments of arrears of £1,125,000.

Another potential source of income for PIK identified by Hudson was an underground fuel hydrant system which had been installed at Prestwick in the early 1960s as part of the airport expansion. The fuelling facilities consisted of three double underground hydrants, six pipelines, and a tank farm, operated by Esso and BP, and partly owned by Shell and BP. In 1991, while Hudson and his team were negotiating with BAA, the authority had been selling off valuable pieces of land adjacent to the airport for what Hudson considered below market value.

BAA then attempted to negotiate an early termination of the Esso lease, which was due to end on December 31, 2000. "During December," said Hudson, "BAA offered to allow Esso out of the remainder of its lease (nine years) for payment of four years' base rent so long as Esso demolished their tanks and filled their hydrant with cement." To Hudson, this was plainly another attempt by BAA to neuter the airport. Esso's in-house solicitor Lesley Galvin, knowing of ACAP's plans to purchase the airport, refused to proceed with BAA. PIK signed the final agreement to buy the airport in February 1992, but as early as September and October the previous year, Hudson had been in touch with both Esso and BP to discover what he could about their situations at the airport, so they were aware of what was going on.

Hudson began his own discussions with Esso in April shortly after taking over and, on August 20, 1992, Esso offered PIK 50% of the remaining basic rent, the £120,000, and they offered to demolish the fuel farm, the same deal turned down in December, but Hudson refused. On studying the leases with Esso, BP and Shell late one night in the offices of McClure Naismith in the last week of March 1992 just before they took over the airport, Hudson had appreciated that he could construct a 'creative scenario' not yet appreciated by the fuelling tenants under which they might be burdened with a range of environmental liabilities, some under the lease and others under other areas of the law. Also, he did not want to be at the mercy of a multi-national fuel supplier. He wanted PIK to be the sole supplier of aviation fuels so that he could entice traffic by offering bargain fuel. Thus, he wanted Esso's tank farm, Esso's hydrants, plus their expertise and goodwill which would help him resurrect the operation and provide training for his own staff. He also wanted them to provide fuel at prices PIK could afford, and allow them to supply at competitive prices.

Negotiations lasted 27 months and by April 1994 Hudson had "imagineered" a deal which gave PIK cash and put the company into the aviation fuelling business, a prerequisite for his next move, the negotiation with BP. Shell having closed its operations some time earlier was to be dealt with last, and in Hudson's plan, potentially the most lucrative section of the operation. As part of the deal with Esso, the fuel company paid PIK cash of £575,000 and Hudson got (a) his fuel supply contract at prices that would allow PIK to compete with BP; (b) 12 months of technical services, including training and safety audits provided by Esso at no cost; (c) two fuel bowsers and three fuelling carts in good repair and condition; (d) a functional fuel hydrant with all tanks tested including ultrasound and in good repair and condition.

Later, after the "BP Treaty" as Hudson called it, the bowsers and carts were sold for £75,000, giving this Esso deal a cash value to the airport of £650,000 plus the value of the hydrant, the tanks and access to the rail siding and pipeline under the highway. The Esso deal was an essential step in Hudson's four part strategy of (a) obtaining low-cost long-term fuel supplied from BP — the only company with a refinery in Scotland and thus the only potential supplier of lowest cost fuel; (b) putting PIK into the fuelling business with a workable hydrant system, vehicles, tanks and a supply of fuel allowing them to effectively shut BP out of the market if it was deemed necessary; (c) converting BP into a partner whose sole role was to provide fuel at attractive pricing and to provide expertise; and (d) gaining working capital from Esso, BP and finally Shell, in increasing amounts.

In the event, having set PIK up in the fuel business with the Esso facilities, Hudson was able to conclude the deal he wanted with BP in late 1996, negotiations he had also started with them in 1992. Through this BP contract, he attained all his goals: long-term supply until the end of 2010 (a 10-year extension); control of the price of fuel and operating costs; lower fuel supply costs than the Esso deal; BP as a partner providing all the commercial experience, the market information, the working capital and taking all credit risks and 50 per cent of the profits on the bulk of the sales. In addition, BP transferred their 100% interests in the rail siding, the rail siding equipment and the pipeline under the A79, their 50% interest in the tank farm and their own hydrant. BP also agreed to pay PIK £718,875 and stop all direct sales of Avgas to the BAe Flying College, thus adding the College to the PIK/BP joint venture customer roster.

To Hudson, the main benefit of the joint venture with BP was that the airport had ultimate control of the price of fuel sold at the airport while running the operational side of the business with BP running the financial side providing all working capital and credit facilities for the purchase of jet fuel and Avgas, health and safety, insurance, commercial expertise and provision of purchaser credit facilities. BP also paid for

Matthew Hudson's multi-functional, multi-skilled, super-enthusiastic employees made Prestwick's workforce the most efficient in the airport business *Photograph courtesy of Phil Toman*

staff uniforms. As Hudson saw it, for balance sheet purposes this deal was worth in the region of £2 million to £3 million to the airport.

Hudson then intended a deal with Shell, the last of the original Seven Sisters lessees. But he was to be overtaken by events.

SPRING 1994 and Prestwick Airport relished the prospect of more passengers. The airport was making money and, in fact, had been in profit in every quarter in the two years since the takeover, thanks to Hudson's stringent approach to management, keeping all the services in-house. The PIK Group was a resounding financial success, based on successful implantation of the pre-acquisition strategic plan enhanced by the effects of Hudson's various contractual negotiations.

The freight plan was becoming more successful each month. The first passengers for a couple of years had flown out to the Algarve on an Air Columbus charter in March, more charter flights were in the pipeline with the busy summer holiday programme ahead, and flights for Florida would take off that November. The next element in the strategic plan was still to be installed, however: the low-cost scheduled flights. The high cost of those flights to London during the takeover negotiations still rankled. Hudson had been chasing the established airlines in Europe without much success. "Airlines are great followers," he said. "They are not leaders, they like to go where others are, like the mass move to Glasgow after Open Skies." So he arranged meetings in America with the presidents of all the main US airlines: American in Dallas, United in Chicago, Delta in Atlanta, Continental, US Airways. The only meeting he was refused was the one he sought with Herb Kelleher, the legendary founder of budget success story Southwest, who was heard over the phone shouting to his secretary: "I don't want to go to f***ing Europe." Kelleher's airline would later be the inspiration for Michael O'Leary's Ryanair and Stelios Haji-Ioannou's easyJet.

Hudson had a clear and detailed strategic plan for using Prestwick as a main gateway into Europe for US flights. He tried to interest the US carriers in using Prestwick as a hub for Europe, using the argument that instead of their planes in a queue circling round Heathrow for an hour, they could have landed at Prestwick one hour before the Heathrow ATC delay and then, with all European formalities cleared, be on their way to the continent on point-to-point smaller regional jets — all this before the Heathrow arrivals had received their luggage. And, he argued, Prestwick was a lot cheaper to use than Heathrow.

"They could have used 757s to cross the ocean, then have regional jets into Europe," said Hudson. "They would have had a wonderful choice, but they were too cowardly to do that. As I said, airlines are great followers." The airlines all said it was a great idea and they would get back to him. "But," said Hudson, "they were worried about angering BAA and their own unions. What would their staff say? Pilots like to go to London. Prestwick was not their scene. What could they do in Scotland if they didn't play golf? I still remember my meeting with the legendary president of American Airlines and his two top lieutenants one of whom, Don Carty, later became president. They were very gracious to me, a nobody with a deserted airport. The president was describing their fight with Southwest in the USA and told me that when Southwest entered one of their markets, they had no choice but to leave. That made me determined to create low-cost flights connecting Scotland to England, Scandinavia and the continent."

The rail station was almost up and open but no scheduled flights were there to be served. Hudson decided to look nearer home, at all routes flying out of Scotland. He asked Hugh Lang, by then his commercial director, to get all the fares for everywhere passengers could go from Glasgow and Edinburgh. He wanted to know the cost-by-seat mile. All were very high, and one of the highest was Dublin out of Glasgow with, as he saw it, the gold being reaped by Aer Lingus. An examination of all the airlines flying in and out of Dublin uncovered a modest little airline called Ryanair.

At the beginning of 1994, Ryanair were flying two million passengers into England from Ireland, but were unknown in Scotland and, in fact, were considered a bit of a joke by the big boys. BA were particularly amused and when flights were negotiated for Stansted Airport they considered it a "pipsqueak airline flying into a tinpot airport in the middle of nowhere," according to Stansted's MD at the time. The description rang bells at Prestwick. Hudson took a closer look at Ryanair. "Their story was that they were the little airline and they were cheap; cheap and nasty. Immediately, I thought:

That's us!" A low-cost airline needs a low-cost airport, he reasoned. Ryanair were a perfect fit for Prestwick. They slotted neatly into the second leg of his passenger strategy: pile it high and sell it cheap.

Coincidentally, Ryanair had been looking to expand their flights into the UK and had heard about Prestwick. Hudson's son Mark was by then working for PIK and he took the initial call from Ryanair. He hurried down the corridor to MD Paddy Healey's office and explained that this small Irish airline were interested in coming to Prestwick.

Hudson flew to Dublin with Healey and his wife Bonnie — it was the couple's home town and they planned to make some family visits during the trip. They flew Aer Lingus out of Glasgow. "Low, slow, bumpy and expensive," was how Hudson described it. It was a very uncomfortable flight on a turbo prop, he said, it never really got up very high, took 35 minutes and cost £240 each, although Bonnie was able to fly half-price because she was a wife. "Disgraceful," said Hudson, "but they could get away with it."

Hudson and Healey arrived at the Ryanair office for what turned out to be many hours of really hard bargaining. The privately-run Prestwick Airport obviously appealed to O'Leary. Hudson told him he was doing everything right for his airline but he had one big cost that he couldn't overcome — the airport. Hudson said: "I am going to give that to you. You can use my airport for NOTHING. Not only that, I won't charge you for air traffic control either." Hudson told him how the airport did everything, that O'Leary wouldn't need staff on the ground. He told him: "From our point of view, all you are doing is driving the bus. I'm doing everything else. You just have to show up. There will be no landing charges, no air traffic control charges, no check-in charge. Nothing. The price per passenger would be a bargain £1.50.

But O'Leary was still suspicious. He said: "You'll just change that after it is successful, I know what you people are like."

So then Hudson gave him a guarantee for five years if he would sign up — but with one catch. "I knew there'd be a f---ing catch," said O'Leary.

Hudson continued: "Here's the catch: when I am right and you are paying me £1.50 for every passenger and you have lots of bums on seats, you can't raise your fares. That's going to be our deal. Free use of my airport for five years, everything included and you're going to keep the fares down and you are going to build up your traffic so much that you will want to base some aircraft at Prestwick and fly other routes."

In the end, a return fare of £55 was the deal hammered out, with two flights a day leaving Prestwick for Dublin, a big improvement on the £240 Aer Lingus charged. Hudson found O'Leary an interesting and charming man, immediately liked him and came to respect his many abilities. They were alike in many ways, aggressive and successful entrepreneurs in their own right, known for not taking any prisoners and not afraid to make enemies on the road to success. O'Leary had a similar background to Hudson. Both worked while at university. O'Leary took a business degree at Trinity then went on to study accountancy, specialising in tax law, but his ambition was to become an entrepreneur and make money. He dabbled in retailing, purchased a newsagent's in the west of Dublin and started investing in property. He left Stokes Kennedy Crowley, one of Ireland's biggest firms, and set out on his own and spent many years "ducking and diving", as he described it — but very successfully.

In 1988, while working for Stokes Kennedy Crowley he had met Tony Ryan of Ryanair, Ireland's "second" airline, when he turned up for an audit of his farm in County Tipperary. Some time later, when Ryan was looking to take on a personal assistant he thought of the young accountant. His chief task was to tackle Ryanair's cost base but the airline continued to lose money in its battle with the protected state airline Aer Lingus and at one time O'Leary recommended that it should be shut down. After the Irish government produced a new policy allowing for two Irish airlines and clearing the way for routes from Dublin to the rapidly-expanding Stansted, the situation began to look up for Ryanair. One day when O'Leary was telling Ryan what he thought should be done with the money-losing airline, his boss said: "If you're so smart why don't you run it?" So O'Leary said, "All right then."

The major change came after O'Leary met Herb Kelleher of Southwest and became convinced that Ryanair should follow that pattern of low fares, no frills and more frequent flights. By 1992 he had turned Ryanair around. It was on a steady flight path and by 1993 O'Leary as chief executive still worked on the ramp moving luggage on busy days but had become a multi-millionaire and was on his own path to aviation history.

Hudson and Healey returned to Prestwick with their done deal, but not everyone was happy with the terms, including Hugh Lang, the airport's commercial director. He had carried out an analysis when Hudson first thought about approaching Ryanair and felt they should charge around £5 a passenger. But to Hudson, getting the passengers in was the priority and he knew he would make the real money from all the ancillary services, all operated by PIK: car parking, restaurants, shops, bars, duty-free, aviation fuel and PIK's own travel agent which they had formed by this time, Skye Travel. "They had a deal and were getting scheduled services," said Lang. "Now, 14 years on, that is how the majority of deals are done with low-cost airlines."

The inaugural Dublin flight was set for May 3, 1994. Prestwick had thrown down the gauntlet to Aer Lingus by offering two flights a day, seven days a week. Hudson decided they had to have a press conference. At that time O'Leary did not do press conferences — in fact he studiously avoided the media spotlight, saying he "couldn't stand journalists". But on this occasion Hudson insisted. As had become the habit, the press conference had to be in Glasgow, still the only way to ensure major media attention, and the Scottish press loved O'Leary, who turned up in his trademark casual look — open-necked shirt and jeans.

"I knew they would love him," said Hudson. "He was so quick and so charming and so refreshing. Mind you, I had warned him to try and not use the F-word."

The chosen venue was an Irish pub and Paddy Healey remembers the day vividly.

Michael O'Leary and Matthew Hudson promote the beginning of Ryanair's cut-price flights from Prestwick to London. The relationship with Ryanair was a game-changer. *Photo courtesy of Phil Toman*

"All the great and the good were there, and standing in the corner were two priests. Matthew asked me what they were doing there. I said to him they are the two most important people in the room. Next Sunday, I told him, they will be telling people from the pulpit that there is this new cheap airline flying to Dublin out of Prestwick. He didn't recognise the Irish way of thinking."

And that was how Ryanair came to Prestwick. In a blaze of publicity.

Hudson was proved right: the Dublin route was an instant success in both directions. The Scots queued in their thousands for the cheap half-hour trip to Dublin, and the Irish did likewise to come and spend weekends and holidays in Scotland. The flights were an immediate boost to both economies. Spurred on by this success, Hudson wanted a low-cost scheduled flight to London. Invitations to tender were sent out emphasising the importance of tourism in Scotland. While British Midland replied to the invitation, saying it was "presumptuous", neither British Airways nor Air UK bothered to reply.

Ryanair, buoyed by the financial success of their single route with a low-cost airport 'partner', showed interest. Hudson overcame O'Leary's hesitation about breaking out of his route model (Dublin to somewhere and return) and they began negotiations with plans to introduce the service that September with a £59 return fare agreed — by far the cheapest London flight on offer from Scotland — with the first flights planned to take off in November, in good time for the Christmas trade. With the added attraction of the free travel from any rail or bus station, thousands rang up to book the cheap seats.

It was not long, however, before the project seemed destined to be grounded before it took off. Ryanair's rivals, who had shown no interest in the service, were conspiring to ground the flights on this lucrative route. As a foreign airline, Ryanair had to set up a separate company in Britain, Ryanair UK, which had to apply for an airline operator's certificate to take off. This would take 10 to 15 weeks and in the interim O'Leary had arranged for GB Airways to lease one of its Boeing 737s to operate the service. It was the use of an Irish-registered plane on an internal UK route that prompted the first objection from rival carriers. They insisted that Ryanair used a British-registered aircraft on the route. At such short notice, Ryanair could only find a smaller BAe 1-11 jet which was potentially calamitous: it would mean that Ryanair would have to leave at least one passenger behind on the inaugural flight and that many who had already booked seats on the new service would have to be turned away.

Memories of the Highland Express launch debacle began to loom. Then British Midland and Air UK, which were both operating Scotland-to-London services out of Glasgow and Edinburgh, objected to a non-UK airline operating an internal service. Although restrictions were due to be removed throughout Europe in two years, the airlines made it clear they would not tolerate any relaxation of the rules ahead of schedule.

British Midland also threatened to sue Ryanair for its "misleading" advertising, which said it flew to Glasgow when they were in fact advertising to Glasgow Prestwick.

Hudson, who of course stood to gain enormously from the scheduled London service, exerted pressure, along with Lord Younger, on the Ministry of Transport to let the service go ahead — and the airline was granted a last-minute dispensation. After days of fraught, high-level political negotiations and crisis management, Ryanair was ready to take off for London from Prestwick on October 27. In the following weeks the airline's UK division would be fully registered to get the operations certificate covering routes in the UK. Hugh Lang, by now the airport managing director, said: "It was touch-and-go whether or not the service would start but we pressed ahead with ticket sales anyway."

Lang felt it was very disappointing that airlines should attempt to stifle competition by any means they could and he was particularly disappointed at the actions of British Midland in threatening legal action as they had always portrayed themselves as champions of competition. Tim Jeans, chief executive of Ryanair, admitted to many sleepless nights before the last-minute political intervention gave the go ahead for take-off. By now there was another competitor on Ryanair's tail, easyJet, flying between Glasgow and Luton. According to Hudson, easyJet founder Stelios initially approached Prestwick as well as Glasgow but by that time they were well into their deal with Ryanair and felt a certain loyalty to O'Leary and easyJet went on to sign their deal with Glasgow.

Competition was already fierce on the Scotland-London route, with some 33,000 passengers flying every week, enjoying the choice of even more airlines. A vicious price war followed with British Midland, the second largest carrier, offering a £58 return ticket for some flights from Glasgow and Edinburgh. British Airways' lowest fare went from £220 to £74. Ryanair was advertising seats at £59 return, but to qualify for the cheapest ticket travellers had to spend a Saturday night or two other nights in London. In a bid to attract more business Ryanair decided to match easyJet's £28 each-way deal and pledged every seat would be available at this price, without restriction.

Ryanair now admit that they found the Prestwick/London route very tricky at the start and they almost abandoned it, which would have spelled disaster for the airport. O'Leary had demanded that any new route would break even in a very short time. He is reported as saying: "Some airlines enter a new route and aim to make a profit in three years. We will not enter a route if we can't break even in three hours and grow the market by at least 100 percent." As a last-ditch effort they decided to add more flights to stimulate demand — and much to their surprise it worked. Ryanair went on to introduce four scheduled flights a day from Prestwick to London. Over the next few years, Ryanair continued to expand at Prestwick. The next destination was into continental Europe, to the small airport at Beauvais, near Paris, with passengers being connected to the city centre by coach. This proved an instant success and was quickly followed by flights to Haan near Frankfurt, Charleroi, outside Brussels and, perhaps the most popular route, Stockholm in Sweden. This route brings thousands of tourists into Scotland, many attracted by the country's golf courses. Ryanair's services are a great boon to Scottish tourism and particularly to Ayrshire.

Hudson has watched with admiration the Ryanair expansion, which he always predicted. He says he encouraged O'Leary to look to Europe, to follow the model of looking for small airports near to large centres. He also supported the Ryanair move to take booking online and talked to him about packaging. "At the start passengers weren't even offered a packet of peanuts on Ryanair flights," said Hudson. "At one point I said to Michael: 'You are missing the boat here. A few more pennies, every little bit counts.'"

He encouraged him to follow the Prestwick Airport model, taking money from every source possible.

Chapter 11
Up, Up...
And Away

PIK

D ESPITE the shaky start, during its first five years of operations, PIK — later to become Prestwick Aviation Holdings
Ltd — had watched its net equity of less than £300,000
rocket to a sum approaching £62 million. Having started
out with 51 employees on the opening day, by December
1996 the figure stood at 330.

In their first full year of operation, ending in March
1993, PIK were pleased to make a profit before depreciation and tax of £874,000.
By November 1995 the group had made a profit of £1.55million. The following
year this had grown to a profit of £2.35 million, the airport contributing £1.185
million and the facilities £1.395 million.

By 1997 the airport was a genuine commercial success, Around 700,000 passengers passed through the airport that year and PIK was competing successfully with Glasgow and Edinburgh. From a deserted hulk with no passengers and
just six freight flights a week, Glasgow Prestwick International was booming.

The airport's business model had even won a prestigious European award and
had its regular scheduled airline, Ryanair, with passengers flying all over Europe;
the freight figures were some of the best in the world; the rail halt was open, the
holiday charter business was good. Through Hudson's simple operating strategy
of running everything themselves and the various deals — taking over the duty-
free, increased parking, operating foreign exchange, the increased MOD leases
and the fuel deals — the PIK net profit was around £3 million. Forecast turnover
for the PIK holdings group in 1997 was £16,730,517.

Hudson felt strongly PIK should not stand still, but must build on its success.
He had by this time moved back to America, living part of the year in Florida,
having moved his family out of their home at Blanefield, and staying in Redcroft,
near Prestwick, when he had to be in Scotland. His plan was to do another Prestwick, with an underused airport in Florida, but his board colleagues were not
so sure. They had seen their investment increase beyond their wildest dreams.
Their initial act of faith, £50,000 from their own pockets, had grown hand-
somely. But they were all getting older. Many were beginning to feel it was time
to sell. Hudson had told them on many occasions that they could not stay just
one little airport, for all kinds of reasons. Managers, he said, needed somewhere
to go, something to aim for. "We had saved the airport for Scotland, put it on a
firm footing. But we needed to expand as a business," he said. The board took a
different view and pointed out that, at 55, Hudson was the youngest on the team.
Hudson's search for a new airport venture would take him away much of the time
and, with the exception of Jim Moffat, the board members said they would prefer
to sell on.

**Previous page: An aerial view of Prestwick Airport, with its rail halt finally in place. This proved to be a
symbolic change to the airport's future.** *Photograph courtesy of Phil Toman*

Hudson reluctantly agreed to go with the board. "I would have been happy not to sell," he said, "but the board were adamant. I would also have been happy to hang on and sell for more, but in the end I was happy to sell for what we did."

The mid-1990s was a time when bus companies were taking over airports in other parts of the world. Hudson and his general manager, Hugh Lang, thought this might be the route to follow and spoke to First Group, then to National Express to establish whether they would be interested and to find out the kind of price they might expect to get. The obvious target was Stagecoach, the hugely-successful Scottish bus company run by the brother-and-sister partnership of Brian Souter and Ann Gloag. Stagecoach would go on to become the second-largest transport firm in the UK, a leading international transport group operating bus, train, tram express coach and ferry interests worldwide, particularly in North America. Hudson wanted to retain the airport business in Scotland, feeling it was important that such an important Scottish asset should go to a Scottish company. Stagecoach had been born of deregulation in the British express coach market in the early 1980s, but its roots can be traced back to 1976 when Ann Gloag and her husband Robin set up a small motor caravan and minibus hire business called Gloagtrotter. Ann's accountant brother Brian Souter joined the firm and expanded the business into bus hire. Robin Gloag subsequently sold his shareholding in the business and ceased any involvement after the collapse of his marriage to Ann. Then the Transport Act 1980 which freed express services of 35 miles and over from regulation by the Traffic Commissioners, brought new opportunities for the Perth-based company.

Services were launched from Dundee to London using second-hand Neoplan coaches. For a while they offered a very personal service with Brian Souter doing the driving and Ann Gloag making up sandwiches and snacks for the passengers, a hint of the Hudson approach to business. Successfully competing against the then state-owned National Express and Scottish Citylink groups, the company grew significantly between 1981 and 1985, when Stagecoach entered local bus operation with the acquisition of McLennan of Spittalfield near their base in Perth. Their early success allowed Stagecoach to take advantage of the privatisation of the national bus groups. Several firms were purchased from the National Bus Company, Scottish Bus Group, London Buses and various city councils. The company consolidated its operations during the 1990s by purchasing management- and employee-owned bus companies, often former NBC and SBG firms where the owners were keen to make a huge profit from their sale. Stagecoach left the long-distance express coach market in 1988 when it sold its operations to National Express.

Controversy was never far from Stagecoach in those early days and the company often found itself on the wrong side of the Competition Commission and facing sharp media criticism over its predatory approach to smaller operators. Bitter "bus wars" broke out in towns and cities throughout Britain as Stagecoach took on the local competition head-first, often forcing the competitors to abandon traditional markets and sometimes causing the collapse of smaller operators. This was through aggressive pricing and timing and often running more buses on a route than necessary, and just a few minutes ahead of the competition.

In Perth, the presence of Stagecoach led the dominant operator, Strathay Scottish, to abandon local services in the town. Similarly, Stagecoach subsidiary Bluebird Buses replaced Highland Scottish buses on most city services in and around Inverness. Equally-aggressive tactics were used to encourage Scottish Citylink into a joint venture. In Darlington, however, they turned the aggression up a few notches when the borough council put Darlington Transport up for sale in 1994. Despite submitting a bid through its Busways subsidiary, Stagecoach lost out to Yorkshire Traction (which was eventually taken over by Stagecoach in 2005). In response, Stagecoach Busways registered identical routes to Darlington Transport and subsequently began operations running free buses across Darlington Transport's network. Yorkshire Traction withdrew its bid and no other interested parties stepped forward. Within a week of Stagecoach arriving in town, Darlington Transport went into receivership and ceased trading. This action would lead the government to reform the regulatory framework for bus operations in the UK.

Eager to find a buyer for Prestwick, Lord Younger, who knew Brian Souter, arranged for him to meet with Hudson in his Royal Bank of Scotland head office in Edinburgh. The two entrepreneurs liked each other immediately. Hudson was impressed, if surprised, by Souter's casual appearance — wearing his trademark track shoes and carrying his traditional plastic bag instead of a briefcase. They quickly agreed they could do business. After a series of negotiations the airport was sold to Stagecoach in early 1998 for £34 million, 95 per cent of which was in Stagecoach shares. By any standards the board members had made a handsome profit from their initial £50,000 investment.

Hudson was reluctant to let go of what he saw as "his" airport and came to a personal agreement with Souter that he would keep a twenty five per cent stake in the company and would still be in charge of operations. He said: "Through this agreement with Brian I was still going to be in control. If I hadn't been going to be in control I would not have been in favour of selling it." His understanding was that his connection with Stagecoach was going to be with Brian himself, but things didn't quite work out that way. Hudson continued: "He didn't mention to me that he was going to appoint a new chief executive to be in charge of the airport end of his business."

Souter had appointed Mike Kinsky, head-hunted from ScottishPower. When Hudson first met Kinsky his reaction was instant antipathy. He knew right away the two of them were not going to get on. Hudson thought he was in charge — that had been his deal with Souter — but the new CEO, who had been human resources director with ScottishPower and who had previous experience in the car industry, immediately began flexing his muscles and insisted he was in charge. He was chief operating officer of Stagecoach group and all the MDs would report to him, he said.

By this time Tom Wilson had been appointed general manager of the airport. He had been promoted from within, having previously been in charge of IT and computer technology under Hudson. Hudson's protégé, Hugh Lang, had not settled within the new management structure and went on to become managing director of Durham and Tees Valley Airports. Hudson was not happy, but he was still chairman of the company and thought with patience — admittedly not his strongest feature — things would settle down and would work out okay.

The first sign of his final break with Prestwick came following a board meeting when Kinsky demanded that Hudson should also report to him. He was an employee of Stagecoach, he was told. "There was no way I was going to report to this guy," said Hudson, "So I said to Brian: 'I know this guy is new and the city wanted you to have a professional manager, but you should not have appointed him.'" Hudson made it clear that it had to be either Kinsky or him and, being a realist in business, Hudson knew the city would not have been happy to see the new CEO resign so soon into his new appointment. So with great reluctance he pulled out of his agreement with Souter. He found, however, that he was still unable to completely let go and he came to an agreement that he would remain a consultant for Prestwick and part of his remit would be to search out new airports to develop in the US.

At this stage, Stagecoach were keen to expand into airports in America, though in the long term the agreement was not fulfilled as Stagecoach lost interest in airport development in the US. Souter and Hudson, however, remain friends to this day, despite Hudson's continuing regret at walking away from his 'baby'. Before long, all the multi-skilling and award-winning practices he had installed were removed and the airport was back to operating very much in the style of the old loss-making BAA days.

Chapter 12
Into A New
World

PIK

STAGECOACH ownership of the airport was short-lived. In 2001, Prestwick Airport was bought by the New Zealand-based Infrastructure and Utilities NZ Ltd, more commonly known as Infratil. The company wanted to extend their activities into Europe and Prestwick was the ideal opener. They later went on to buy Kent airport and Lubeck in Germany. Initially, Infratil joined forces with Omniport plc, a Scottish company headed by local businessman Bill Barr — who had been unsuccessful in 1992 in joining the PIK consortium. Omniport had a number of Scottish investors and had been formed to establish a network of regional airports. but its connection was short-lived. Omniport disposed of its investment in Prestwick in 2003, though Barr retained his seat on the board.

Prestwick is now solely owned by Infratil Airport Europe and is widely-recognised as one of the fastest-growing airports in the UK with two and a half million passengers passing through every year. In 2005 the company completed a £3 million refurbishment of the terminal buildings — an investment welcomed locally — but one that wasn't without controversy.

The rebranding slogan selected by the new owners was the phrase "Pure Dead Brilliant". Not such a brilliant choice, as it turns out. Reputedly suggested by a junior member of staff, Pure Dead Brilliant, as everyone in the west of Scotland knew — but the management of the airport obviously did not — is pure Glasgow patter, and *outdated* Glasgow patter at that. And given the local history between the Glasgow and Prestwick airports in the past, to the locals it was an ill-advised choice with no Ayrshire connotations. In their defence the management could probably have argued the airport WAS called Glasgow Prestwick — the decision taken by Matthew Hudson in the early days when, being a pragmatist, he realised Glasgow was better known worldwide than Prestwick. And he also knew it would annoy the hell out of BAA's "Abbotsinch" management.

Despite criticism in the local community and the press, the airport stuck to their guns — they had spent a fortune on the rebranding and the slogan was on everything from the terminal frontage to the T-shirts worn by staff. Even the ribbons holding the staff passes carried the slogan.

However the controversy did not end there. The artwork backing up the rebranding showed cartoon Scottish characters and the illustration for the new bar showed a kilted drunk lying unconscious, whisky bottle by his side. Not the right image for the world to see — particularly in a country becoming more aware of drink-related problems. Not funny, said the authorities

Again the airport management stuck to their guns. The image, they said was "fun and visually stimulating". That, however, wasn`t how the local licensing

Previous page: Polish-based Wizz Air was one of many airlines flying out of Prestwick as budget travel boomed at the beginning of the century *Photograph courtesty of Damien McCoy, dmccoy@nildram.co.uk*

authority saw it and when it became clear that sticking with the image could lead to them having their drinks licence withdrawn, management at Prestwick Airport bowed to the mounting pressure.

In 2007 Infratil continued their refurbishment of the terminal buildings, with new shops, bar and restaurant – and the only Starbucks south of Glasgow.

Today Ryanair is still Prestwick's biggest customer, flying to 27 routes all over Europe. Wizzair is flying to four destinations in Polands – one of the fastest growing services – and talks are going on with airport CEO Mark Rodwell about future expansion.

Rodwell, an Australian, took over the management of Prestwick in January 2006 and, much like Matthew Hudson 14 years previously, saw his first job as putting a new management structure in place. With 25 years experience in the aviation industry behind him – he had been manager terminals at Sydney Airport with responsibility for the international terminal before coming to Prestwick as chief executive – he knew he had to build a strong team around him. Three years on, he believes he has one. "I can now step back and get involved in strategic aspects of business as well," he says. He has faced all sort of challenges, not least of which have been the increased security measures after the terrorist attack on Glasgow Airport in July 2007.

He is looking to expand Ryanair business but insists that any new business "must wash its face". Ryanair are notorious for driving hard bargains. As Mark says: "Michael O'Leary's adage is that he will deliver passengers but does not expect to be charged anything by airports. It is up to the airports to make their money from the passengers." An arrangement Hudson helped initiate.

However, Rodwell admits that Prestwick would not be where it is today had it not been for the deal done between Matthew Hudson and Michael O'Leary in 1994.

New markets are opening up all the time, says Rodwell, mainly in eastern Europe, but he does hold out hope for transatlantic services coming back to Prestwick as the low-cost airlines set their sights on destinations further afield.

He sees hard times ahead for the aviation industry, with increased fuel costs and increased competition, but Infratil, he says, is very well placed to meet these challenges. He is optimistic for the future of Prestwick and sees a continued growth in aviation despite all the challenges – financial, environmental and security. "People still travel by air and they will continue to do so," he says.

Freight is still vital to Prestwick's success. It had been on the decline for a few years but 2007 saw an upturn in business. One contributing fact was the huge Polar Air Cargo maintenance facility – one of the success stories of the Stagecoach era and a personal triumph for David Mullen, who had played an important role in the early days of the initial takeover in 1992. Mullen retired from Fedex in 1996 but after a short stint as a consultant he was approached by Polar Air to drive up their quality. It was to be a three-to-six month contract – he was still there in 2006.

One day, Mullen was having a cup of coffee with the Polar director of maintenance, who was passing through the airport on his mission to find a suitable site for a maintenance hangar somewhere in the world. Mullen asked if he had considered Prestwick — and that started a chain of events. Ann Gloag, Stagecoach boss, was approached and her response was immediate. She said: "Build it." Unfortunately, the worldwide economic situation in the summer of 2008 saw the facility close with the ensuing loss of business and jobs.

Other important business for the airpor is in corporate jet aircraft, which is seeing an increase in demand, the military, though HMS Gannet continues to be downgraded and, of course, pilot training. With its good weather record and long runway the airport continues to be a training centre for many major airlines.

The future certainly looks positive for Prestwick.

But none of it would have happened if it hadn't been for the determination of local MP George Younger, the foresight and courage of the group of local businessmen, the support, moral and financial of the local councils, the willingness of the airport staff to adapt to radical changes in work practices and a cut in wages — and the incisive skill, stubbornness and determination of a Canadian lawyer who had come to Scotland for a quiet life. The team who took control in that bold and brave move in 1992 saved Prestwick Airport for the nation.

Yet despite their pivotal roles in saving Prestwick Airport from closure, neither George Younger nor Matthew Hudson were ever formally recognised by authorities in Scotland or the Scottish Office for their efforts. There is no plaque to mark the spot as in the case of the airport founder David McIntyre.

There have been the criticisms — no doubt tinged with envy — that the board members, particularly Matthew Hudson, made personal fortunes from the sale of the airport to Stagecoach. But they had taken the risk. Reported in today`s financial climate no one would blink at such a transaction — similar buyout deals take place all the time.

George Younger died in March 2003 after a long illness and Matthew Hudson lives in West Virginia, USA with his wife Pamela and two youngest children, Amelia and Matthew.

Prologue

A T THE end of October 2008 Mark Rodwell, CEO of Glasgow Prestwick, introduced a draft Master Plan for the airport — taking it well into 2033 and instilling a vote of confidence in its future. Developments underway for early 2009 include a £1.7 million expansion of the departure lounge, a bigger retail space and an expansion of the check-in area.

The future grand plan includes extending the terminal building, new aprons, a car park development and eventually a hotel adjacent to the airport — a concept which was part of the original plans when the current terminal was constructed in the early 1960s. The airport recently acquired the former golf range for additional parking — a piece of land the PIK board fought hard for years to buy after BAA had sold it off at a bargain price in 1990.

Taking Matthew Hudson's vision for the airport a stage further, Mark Rodwell is looking for a working partnership with the integrated travel systems in south west Scotland to increase the reliance on rail travel. This would include an improved rail service linking with Glasgow and Edinburgh, more and larger trains with plenty of baggage space, and a new station. With environmental concerns in mind, he sees 30 per cent of the airport's passengers using the train to get to Prestwick.

The future of the second runway is being looked at — it is used rarely and the space could be developed, perhaps for parking. But Infratil are aware of the sensitivities around such a proposal and are considering many options.

Infratil are confident that Prestwick Airport has a vibrant future — they are looking over the next 25 years to increase the passenger numbers from the current 2.4 million per annum to 11.9 million, and freight rising to 101,000 tonnes per annum

All their proposals were due to go out to consultation around the beginning of 2009, particularly with the local community, who, it appears, will again have a say in the development of their airport.

The final plan was due to be unveiled in the spring of 2009.

As this book went to publication it looked as if BAA might be forced to put Glasgow Airport up for sale after a report by the Competition Commission which was concerned about the company's market dominance in the UK. It recommended three airports be sold and Glasgow looked the favoured choice in Scotland. Rodwell has confirmed that Infratil would be interested in putting in an offer for Prestwick's rival, should the opportunity arise. Now wouldn't that be the final irony?

Acknowledgments

THIS is an account of the saving of Prestwick Airport by the community — for the community, and the country. The story has been put together from many hours of interviews and conversations with employees past and present. I would like to thank the surviving board members and former staff who dug into the recesses of their minds to remember back to the exciting events of 1990-1998; also employees and former councillors of Kyle and Carrick District Council who gave willingly of their time.

I would like to particularly mention Matthew Hudson, recognised — by friend and foe — as the saviour of the airport, who welcomed me complete with tape recorder to his home in West Virginia; Bill Miller, who along with MP George Younger, had the original idea of a private buyout and who also suggested writing a book to tell their story; Allan MacDonald, former MD of British Aerospace at Prestwick, without whose help and knowledge of the history of the site, the buyout would not have been possible; and Dougal McIntyre, whose book about his father's vision, *Prestwick's Pioneer*, was a particularly useful source.

— ANN GALBRAITH, December, 2008

ANN Galbraith is a former editor of the Ayr Advertiser, Scotland's oldest local newspaper. During the 1980s the newspaper backed the campaign to save Prestwick Airport when it was threatened with closure, despite the fact that the newspaper's owner headed the Glasgow business campaign to have the transatlantic flights transferred to that city's airport — dealing a mighty blow to Prestwick.

She lives in South Ayrshire with four cats and is currently a councillor with South Ayrshire Council and a member of the Prestwick Airport Consultative Committee.